South Dublin Libraries

www.southdublinlibraries.ie

D1345769

Lives of the Musicians

Prince

Jason Draper

Laurence King Publishing

LAURENCE KING

First published in Great Britain in 2021 by
Laurence King Publishing
an imprint of The Orion Publishing Group Ltd
Carmelite House, 50 Victoria Embankment
London EC4Y 0DZ

An Hachette UK Company

10 9 8 7 6 5 4 3 2 1

A CIP catalogue record for this book is
available from the British Library.

ISBN: 978 1 91394 755 2

Typeset by Marie Doherty
Printed in Italy by Printer Trento S.r.l.

Laurence King Publishing is committed to ethical
and sustainable production. We are proud participants
in The Book Chain Project®
bookchainproject.com

**BOOK
CHAIN
PROJECT**

www.laurenceking.com
www.orionbooks.co.uk

Cover illustration: Uli Knörzer

CONTENTS

Prologue:
His Royal Badness

lvis Presley was the 'King of Rock'n'Roll' and Michael Jackson the 'King of Pop'. Madonna – Her Madgesty – took the crown as pop's queen. The music world has seen a 'Queen of Soul' (Aretha Franklin), a 'Lizard King' (Jim Morrison) and Beyoncé 'Queen Bey' Knowles, who is married to Shawn 'Jay-Z' Carter, one of many rappers who have declared themselves 'King of New York'. But while these icons had their titles bestowed upon them, or appointed themselves heirs to the throne, Prince was born into his place in the royal pantheon, with a natural ability that seemed to transcend the rules that govern ordinary lives.

Pop, rock, funk and soul – and beyond music into cinema, dance and fashion – Prince conquered them all with a refusal to accept any restrictions on his creative expression. 'To have the theatrical sense of a David Bowie, but to have the virtuoso sense of a Miles Davis and the pop-culture sense of a Madonna – to combine all of that in one person … The compositions are great, but the concept – the whole package – is what's unique,' says Hans-Martin Buff, Prince's engineer in the mid- to late 1990s.

A rarity in the entertainment industry, Prince didn't move to New York or Los Angeles to find fame. Staying in his hometown of Minneapolis, he brought the world to him, turning the 'Minneapolis sound' into a global phenomenon. 'He was coming up at a time when barriers were starting to be broken down,' says Andrea Swensson, author of *Got to Be Something Here: The Rise of the Minneapolis Sound.* 'In town, there were more integrated bands. Nationally, more Black artists were starting to cross over. It was this combination of being in a place that gives you that perspective and drive, and then being at the right time for that drive to actually break through a wall.'

Rescuing himself from poverty and a broken home, Prince made the very act of living an expression of his artistic purpose. 'He completely dedicated himself to his music,' says Lisa Coleman, keyboardist in The Revolution, the band Prince shot to worldwide fame with in the mid-1980s. 'And not just the music – the whole package of being a pop star. Going shopping was almost as important as going to rehearsal. He was really sure about what he was doing. It was kind of mysterious, like: will it work? Who knows? But the fact that he was practising it every day kind of made it inevitable.'

A virtuoso musician who wrote era-defining songs; a wilful enigma who bared his soul through his art; a visionary who could seemingly manifest the impossible into reality – Prince was many things to many people, but everyone who fell into his orbit agrees on one thing: Prince was a genius. But 'to say he's a musical genius is really to miss the point', says Van Jones, a former advisor to President Barack Obama who worked with Prince on secret philanthropic ventures during the 2010s. 'He had a genius for humanity that was so complex it can only express itself musically.' In the years following his death in 2016, that complexity is still being unravelled in order to be fully understood.

'All the way along, he was planting seeds and leaving hieroglyphics and hidden messages and things like that,' says Lisa Coleman. 'He was just becoming a legend and he was writing the story that it was going to be when it was done.'

This is that story.

1

The Kid

'**M**y mother's eyes. That's the 1st thing [eye] can remember,' Prince wrote in his posthumously published memoir, *The Beautiful Ones*. There was 'nothing more beautiful': they were 'playful', promising 'fun & mischief'. The first thing he remembered hearing was his father's piano – 'a joyous sound'.

Mattie Della Shaw was a jazz singer – vivacious, outgoing, always looking for a good time. She already had a son, Alfred, from a previous marriage when she met John L. Nelson at Minneapolis's Phyllis Wheatley House, a community centre for the city's Black population. Sixteen years her senior, John L. was a jazz pianist, the sharply dressed leader of a local outfit, The Prince Rogers Trio. Mattie had a voice like Billie Holiday's, and Nelson asked her to join his group. But while Mattie wanted 'adventure & traveling', John L., who also had four children of his own from a first marriage – Sharon L., Norrine P., Lorna and John R. – wanted to 'make sure there was food on the table'. For Prince, his parents' opposing personalities would take seed within him, as if planting the roots for all that would follow: a lifetime of embodying contradictions in the creation of a unique worldview expressed through his music.

* * * * *

'I called my son Prince because I wanted him to do everything I wanted to do,' John L. told *A Current Affair* in 1991. Growing up in Minneapolis, where he was born at Mount Sinai Hospital on 7 June 1958, nine months after his parents' wedding, the young Prince Rogers Nelson was almost uniquely placed to fulfil that dream. But by the time Prince's sister, Tyka, came along two years later, John L. would feel his own ambitions slipping away.

A pragmatic man with a temper that spilled into the Nelsons' domestic life, he held down two jobs in order to make ends meet: working as a plastic moulder at Honeywell Electronics by day, where he was, reportedly, the first Black employee at the company, and performing in the north-side community centres and downtown strip joints at night, where racist restrictions in the clubs on Hennepin Avenue forced his band to play behind a curtain. Mattie, meanwhile, gave up singing altogether. Looking after a household of two combined families, childcare became her full-time responsibility.

If genetics handed him a mix of his parents' personalities, Prince also inherited a mixed racial bloodline: Mattie had traces of Black, Native American and white ancestry, while John L. was a Black–Italian mix. With the Nelsons making their home at 915 Logan Avenue North, Prince grew up in a small Black community practically quarantined in the north of the city by three highways that cut through the Twin Cities of Minneapolis and Saint Paul. 'The Black community of the time was two per cent of the metro area, but all living in close proximity to one another because of segregation,' Minneapolis music historian Andrea Swensson says. 'North

Minneapolis is this little triangle that's cut off on all sides. It's maybe one by two miles … So you have a community that's completely sequestered, which allowed for a really strong culture to develop.' It was in this small pocket that Prince would encounter many of the musicians that would help him put Minneapolis on the map, among them André Anderson (later known as André Cymone) and Morris Day.

Briefly bussed to Kenwood Elementary as part of a city-wide programme to foster integration, Prince began to interact with more affluent white culture. He would also experience overt racism; unhappy at Kenwood, he transferred to John Hay Elementary, closer to the Nelsons' home in North Minneapolis. 'I was very lucky to be born here, because I saw both sides of the racial issue, the oppression and the equality,' he later said. 'I got the best of all worlds here. I saw what happens here, and it's not like what happens in, say, Atlanta.'

Local radio also helped Prince bridge the cultural divide. In the strictly segregated music industry, Black and white artists were marketed to their own audiences, with little opportunity to cross over. Living within reach of KUXL's mile-radius broadcast signal, Prince was able to tune into the only Black radio station in the area. 'It was a community-run station,' Swensson says. 'The primary programming during the day was religious.'

In the afternoon, however, the influential Minneapolis DJ Jack Harris would take over. Supporting the city's R&B acts, he also spun Motown and Aretha Franklin records alongside cuts by some of Prince's key inspirations, such as Sly & The Family Stone and James Brown. When KUXL went off air at sundown, Prince would turn the dial to KQRS, where he discovered white pop, rock and progressive music, including two more of his lasting influences, Santana and Joni Mitchell. Absorbing all of it, Prince later told *Rolling Stone*, 'I was brought up in a Black and white world ... I always said that one day I was gonna play all kinds of music, and not be judged for the colour of my skin, but the quality of my work.'

The Nelsons attended the Seventh Day Adventist Church, which also brought its influence to bear on the young talent in the making. Although Prince's religious beliefs evolved over the years, he always had a gut-level faith: 'Early on, [eye] believed another power greater than myself was at work in my life,' he would write. As a child, however, he was more interested in the music that church had to offer. 'The most I got out of that was the experience of the choir.' Rather than study the Bible, Prince preferred to spend his time discussing music with a new friend, André Anderson, just three weeks his junior. The youngsters were amazed to discover that André's father, Fred, had played bass with Prince's dad. His mother, Bernadette, was a matriarchal figure in the community who organized youth events.

Arguably the most epochal event for Prince during these years was when, aged five, he was taken to see his father's band perform. 'Artists have the ability 2 change lives with a single per4mance,' he would later reflect, and as John L. led his trio amid a troupe of dancing girls, Prince realized the power that music – and a bandleader – could have on an audience. Five years later, following his parents' divorce, a similar experience confirmed this epiphany: Prince's new stepfather lifted him onto the stage at a James Brown concert, where Prince danced until a bodyguard took him off. 'He inspired me because of the control he had over his band,' Prince said of the 'Godfather of Soul' in 1998, 'and because of the beautiful dancing girls he had. I wanted both.' In his early adolescence, Prince would continue to sneak into clubs in order to watch his father play, racing home before John L. could find out.

Aspiring to match, and even outdo, his father musically and, later, sartorially, Prince would sit at the piano in the front room, teaching himself how to play TV themes – *Batman*, *The Man from U.N.C.L.E.* – in defiance of the house rules: don't touch the instrument. As young as three or four, he'd shake loose from his mother during shopping trips in order to 'jump on the radio, the organ, any type of instrument', Mattie later recalled. 'I'd have to hunt for him, and that's where he'd be – in the music department.'

Although influenced by his jazz-playing father, Prince developed a less abstract playing style better suited to writing pop songs. His first song, often referred to as 'Funk Machine' (though likely just titled 'Machine'), was completed when he was seven. It took his father moving out of the house at around the same time before he could start using the piano freely. Mattie and John L.'s clash of personalities had become too strong for the marriage to endure: 'several breakdowns of communication & even occasional violence' led to their separation, Prince recalled, with one harrowing incident leading Mattie to hold her son up 'as a buffer' between herself and her husband.

'[Eye] had no idea what impact that would have on me,' Prince later wrote of the split, though music provided an escape from the turmoil of his home life: 'Some secrets r so dark they have 2 b turned in2 song 1st b4 one can even begin 2 unpack them.' Years later, in the early 1990s, he would explore themes of domestic violence and child abuse in songs like 'Papa', which ended with a warning (or perhaps affirmation of survival): if you abuse children, they'll turn out like Prince. Another song, 'The Sacrifice of Victor', alluded to his childhood epilepsy: seizures that began at the age of three, but which seem to have subsided around the time of the Nelsons' divorce, and following what Prince later described to his mother as a visitation from an angel who told him he would not be sick any more.

Despite their fractious relationship, Prince still idolized his father, and took an immediate dislike to his new step-father, Hayward Baker, who introduced new punishments, such as locking Prince in a closet ('The best thing that can be said about him was that he made my mother happy').

Aged twelve, and with Mattie giving birth to a new half-brother, Omarr, Prince relocated to his father's nearby studio apartment – where the instruments were – before John L. bought a larger house at 539 Newton Avenue. It was a short-lived arrangement that came to an end when he allegedly found his newly teenaged son fooling around with a girl. Failing to convince his father to take him back, Prince asked his younger sister, Tyka, to intervene on his behalf. She relayed John L.'s message: all Prince had to do was apologize. Prince called again, delivered the apology – and John L. still said no. 'I sat crying at that phone booth for two hours,' Prince told *Rolling Stone* in 1985, in an unusually unguarded statement, adding, 'That's the last time I cried.'

Next was a spell living with his aunt Olivia, in South Minneapolis, which, with his hormones on high alert, may have been misguided. For one, Olivia's devoutly religious household was at odds with her adolescent nephew's new lifestyle; puberty hit Prince 'with the strength of a hurricane & all [eye] could really think about was the opposite sex'. He once claimed his mother supplied him with copies of *Playboy* and other 'erotic literature', in lieu of having 'The Talk'. In his memoir, he placed that responsibility on Hayward, recalling a trip they took with other neighbour-hood kids to watch 'a raggedy R-rated drive-in movie', still avoiding 'The Talk' while letting the action speak for itself. But also, there was no piano in Olivia's home. Feeling sorry, John L. bought Prince a guitar, which he immediately mastered, learning not just how to play the instrument, but how to perform the solos he heard on the latest rock hits.

Prince's next home would allow him to develop his two greatest interests – music and girls – more or less uninhib-ited. Mattie had developed a deep friendship with Bernadette Anderson; the two mothers not only 'had each other's back when it came 2 their husbands', but also shared another arrangement, as Prince later wrote: 'If I die you take care of my children, if you die I take care of yours.' In need of a surrogate family, Prince settled with the Andersons on 1244 Russell Avenue, first sharing a room with his friend André, the youngest of their six children, before resettling to more private quarters in the basement, where he would live for the majority of his teenage years.

Back before Mattie and John L. broke up, 'there were 2 Princes in the house where we lived', Prince wrote. Mattie called John L. 'Prince', after his band, and nicknamed her son Skipper, 'because he was small in size and he was just real cute'.

As an adult, Prince would grow to just five feet two inches – or, as he told people, five foot three. He'd been a talented basketball player, but by the time he enrolled in Minneapolis's Central High his classmates were beginning to outstrip him in size. Prince gravitated even more towards music. Arriving early each day to spend time alone with the instruments in the school's music room, he also persuaded his music teacher to reserve the room for him at lunchtimes.

Practice became a refuge – from other teachers who confused his name with 'Price', and kids who teased him about his clothes (platform shoes, flares and dress shirts with large, pointed collars), his hair ('the biggest afro in the world', according to one schoolmate) and his name ('Princess' was a popular taunt). 'People would say something about our clothes or the way we looked or who we were with, and we'd end up fighting,' he later told *Rolling Stone*. 'I was a very good fighter … I never lost. I don't know if I fight fair, but I go for it.'

Free to explore his natural gift for music, Prince learned how to play most instruments himself, including a brief attempt at the saxophone, which he abandoned after finding it hurt his lip. Back at the Andersons', he split his time between furthering his skills as a musician and gaining experience with the opposite sex, he and André using the basement for more than just band practice.

After cycling through several names – among them Phoenix and, in an early display of the carnality that would dominate his music, Sex Machine – Prince's first band settled on a conflation of two of his favourite groups: Grand Funk Railroad and Graham Central Station (led by another musical idol, former Sly & The Family Stone bassist Larry Graham). With Prince fronting the band on guitar, Grand Central's line-up was rounded out with André Anderson on bass, André's sister Linda on keyboards and Prince's second cousin Charles Smith on drums. When William Doughty and Terry Jackson joined on percussion, the group moved rehearsals from the basement to Jackson's house, next door, where a larger space accommodated sessions that lasted up to six hours.

'In order to thrive economically, they had to appeal to the broader white audience,' Swensson says. 'So for Prince and his peers, that meant learning all of the hits of the day ... and then putting together setlists that they could play at a prom at an all-white high school.' They worked up a repertoire that included funk, rock and pop music. One estimate counted anywhere between two hundred and three hundred songs by the time the group disbanded, including numbers by Jimi Hendrix, Ohio Players, Grand Funk Railroad and Chicago, with original material entering as the band grew in confidence.

Prince also developed his taste in fashion. Reacting against his poverty, he promised himself he would never dress 'raggedy', and cultivated a feminine look with scarves and silk shirts that helped him stand out. Thrift stores were raided in search of fringed vests and boots that recalled the ones favoured by Carlos Santana; when the types of clothes he wanted weren't available, girls would help make outfits for him.

'In Minneapolis, it was cool to be glamorous,' says Lisa Coleman, who, in 1980, would join Prince's band as a keyboardist and move to the city from Los Angeles. More used to the punk sensibility of LA's underground scene, she discovered that going to a club in Minneapolis meant 'you'd want to dress up and not dress down'.

Aided by Bernadette and a local manager, Frank Jackson, Grand Central played wherever they could get bookings: proms, homecomings, the Minnesota State Fair, community centres like The Way – a Black-owned organization that provided space for many of Minneapolis's young musicians to learn their craft – and even neighbours' back gardens. The Phyllis Wheatley Community Center hosted battle-of-the-bands nights where the prize was local fame.

'I don't even know that they were all billed as battle-of-the-bands,' Swensson says. 'I think they saw every concert they played together as a battle. There's just this competitive nature that they all shared.' With Grand Central, Prince would take to the stage to prove himself against a host of outfits, some of whose members would become significant collaborators in the future: The Family (with bassist Sonny Thompson, later of The New Power Generation), Mind & Matter (led by future keyboardist with The Time, Jimmy 'Jam' Harris) and Flyte Tyme (featuring another future Time musician, Terry Lewis, on bass). 'They wanted to come out on top and get the most claps and cheers and adoration, and prove to other artists that they had rehearsed the hardest and were the best.'

In 1974, cousin Charles's sports interests were distracting from his band duties, so he was replaced by another classmate, Morris Day, whose mother, LaVonne Daugherty, would also play a part in Prince's burgeoning career. LaVonne hustled for the band, now renamed Grand Central Corporation, scoring gigs, paying for demo recordings, trying to secure a record deal. Another family connection, Pepé Willie, husband of Prince's cousin Shauntel Manderville, was brought in to help the operation. Soon realizing who the group's stand-out talent was, Willie enlisted Prince as a session musician for his own group, 94 East. Contributing guitar, synthesizers, keyboards and drums, and earning a co-write on the song 'Just Another Sucker', Prince finally entered a professional studio.

The band changed their name to Champagne (similarities with Graham Central Station had become too obvious to ignore) and began recording together at Moon Sound Studios, a small facility run by local concert promoter and advertising-jingles writer Chris Moon. He, too, homed in on Prince as their leading light. For his eighteenth birthday, in 1976, the same year that he gave his first ever interview, to the *Central High Pioneer* ('I really feel that if we had lived in Los Angeles or New York or some other big city, we would have gotten over by now'), Prince received the keys to the studio. In return for helping Moon develop some of his own songs, he could have as much free recording time as he wanted.

* * * * *

LaVonne, meanwhile, had piqued the interest of Isaac Hayes – the Black Moses himself, Stax Records's flagship artist and the man behind the *Shaft* theme tune, a song that defined a strain of funk music in the 1970s. Hayes considered offering the group a deal. But Prince, feeling that he could work faster on his own, left the band. André wasn't far behind, and so a renamed Shampayne lost its sparkle.

Prince, too, had refined his name, dropping 'Nelson'. His one-word description in the Central High graduation book read 'music' – Moon Sound was a full-time gig, if not yet a money-maker. Although he was broke, and would later recall standing outside McDonald's just so he could 'smell stuff', Prince took his fee from a recording session with The Family, where he provided guitar and backing vocals to their song 'Got to Be Something Here', and bought a plane ticket east. Staying with his older half-sister Sharon, he shopped a demo around New York, looking for a solo deal. Tiffany Entertainment offered to buy the publishing rights to the songs, but Prince, having studied some business of music at school, had an early understanding of the importance of owning his work and turned them down.

A call from Minneapolis had him on the plane home. After some convincing from Chris Moon, Owen Husney, the head of a local advertising company, had listened to the demo. He thought it was the work of a group of musicians – a Black singer fronting a fusion of R&B, pop, rock and soul by a band that 'crossed many barriers where most artists of the day either refused to go, or just plain lacked the ability to get there', he recalled in his memoir. Husney wanted to put his resources into becoming Prince's full-time manager and securing him a deal.

He found an apartment for the young star in the city's Uptown district, near his own office. 'Uptown is the hipster neighbourhood,' Swensson says. 'Back then it was very white. It was where the punk rock bands were.' Living within walking distance of their favourite bars and record stores, Prince had 'moved into a different scene'. Booked in at Minneapolis's Sound 80 studio with local engineer David Rivkin (brother of Bobby Rivkin, who would soon become Prince's drummer), Prince taught himself to use the top-of-the-line synths and recorded a new demo. Husney put it in an all-black press pack that featured just the artist's name on the front in order to create mystique.

Playing the labels off against each other to create a buzz was easy; convincing them to give in to Prince's demands for full creative control – from the way he was presented down to how his albums were recorded – was not. As RSO, ABC/Dunhill, A&M and CBS all left the running, either uninterested or unwilling to agree to the terms Husney offered, Warner Bros became their last option. They 'didn't do the safe stuff', Marylou Badeaux says; she was then working in radio promotion in the Black music department, on her way to becoming the division's Vice President of Special Projects. 'They were into the music. Into creativity. Into things that maybe the next label wouldn't be comfortable with … And they weren't afraid of the fact that this punk kid comes in and says, "I will not be labelled a Black artist. And I'm gonna produce my own albums. I'm gonna play all the instruments."'

Rather than try to impress Prince and Husney with freebies and fancy dinners, Warner Bros's head of pop promotion, Russ Thyret, took them to his house, sat on the floor and talked music with them. Thyret 'saw something' in the teenager, Badeaux confirms. Legendary label execs Mo Ostin and Lenny Waronker concurred. They were willing to offer an unprecedented three-album deal that allowed Prince to co-produce his music.

Husney called it the biggest deal of 1977 and the most lucrative offer ever made for an unknown artist. Convinced that Warner Bros would offer him the best chance to be heard in the way he wanted, on 25 June 1977, less than three weeks after his nineteenth birthday, Prince signed with the label that would release some of his greatest music and provoke his most bitter disputes. For now, however, there was a deal to celebrate in the way he knew best: with the ink barely dry, Prince was back in Minneapolis, in Sound 80, recording a new song dedicated to creative and business partnerships: 'We Can Work It Out'.

2

Sex Defender

P rince had the final word on every element of his music, from writing and performing most of the songs himself to producing the albums and conceptualizing the artworks and promo videos. Rehearsals were legendarily gruelling affairs, with Prince drilling his musicians for hours, overwhelming them with song arrangements, choreography and coded phrases or gestures that could signal a change at any point on stage. 'Produced, Arranged, Composed and Performed by Prince' was the line on most of his record sleeves, but that applied also to his entire lifestyle, lived, as it was, with the same tight control.

With so many ideas pouring out of him, he had to work fast to capture them all; to express every facet of himself with an artistic integrity few could match. Finishing songs in a day, Prince had little patience for processes that slowed him down: technological limitations; tape machines that couldn't wind fast enough; other musicians, incapable of learning parts quicker than he could record them himself. If, sonically speaking, some of his albums could have been more polished, they nevertheless had an immediacy that jumped out of the speakers – far more preferable than overworking an idea and draining the life out of it.

As Susan Rogers, Prince's studio engineer throughout his commercial peak, from 1983 to 1987, says, he was an 'extraordinary virtuoso' who would 'go from instrument to instrument so quickly that the end product looked like perfectionism … not because he worked to make it perfect; it was perfect because he was that good'. Cutting corners as they recorded, prioritizing capturing a feeling over everything else, Rogers notes that 'the sound of those records wasn't that great. What was great about them was the ideas and the playing.'

Prince learned this the hard way.

* * * * *

What Prince expected from those around him was no different to the demands he placed on himself. Rehearsing in Husney's office, he remained resolutely focused on his new music. 'Anyone around then knew what was happening,' Prince later recalled of the period leading up to his debut album. 'I was *working*. When they were sleeping, I was *jamming*. When they woke up, I had another groove.'

But even keeping up with his own relentless pace took its toll during the recording of his debut. By Prince's own admission, he was 'a physical wreck' after the sessions. Warner Bros may have allowed their teenage wunderkind to take on co-production duties, but when they suggested that Maurice White, of Earth, Wind & Fire, oversee the sessions alongside him, Prince balked against the label's attempt to turn him into the next disco hitmaker. 'Don't make me Black,' he cautioned them, adding, 'My idols are all over the place.' Prince was serving notice: he wanted to be marketed like other mainstream – white – artists.

To prove he could handle his own production, Prince spent a day in Amigo Studios, in Los Angeles, recording 'Just As Long As We're Together' as part of a live audition – only he was unaware he was under observation and mistook the label execs that drifted in and out for janitors. Satisfied that their new signing knew his way around the equipment, Warner Bros dropped the Maurice White idea, but installed the experienced Tommy Vicari as executive producer, just in case.

Prince's debut album was recorded at the Record Plant in Sausalito, just north of San Francisco, from October through December 1977. Prince, Vicari, Owen Husney and Husney's wife Britt rented a three-storey house in Corte Madera, overlooking the San Francisco Bay, though Prince hardly hung around enough to enjoy the view. Still only a teenager, he pushed everything – himself included – to the limit, often working from 3pm to 5am in his determination to succeed.

Prince barely spoke to Vicari and treated him like an unwanted babysitter, rolling his eyes at suggestions, drawing caricatures of him in the margins of studio notes and pushing the producer away from the recording console once he'd observed anything he needed to learn. Back at the apartment, Prince tormented Vicari with practical jokes, rousing the increasingly exhausted producer from sleep – where he was relegated to the sofa – in order to take unflattering photos of him.

When his Minneapolis friends André Anderson and David Rivkin were flown out to the sessions, Prince relaxed

– a little. Although he wouldn't let André perform on the album, he felt more comfortable recording his vocals with Rivkin, an engineer he trusted. Meanwhile, Prince had 'absorbed everything he needed out of Tommy Vicari's brain', Husney recalled. 'Tommy was heartbroken, because he had just been treated like shit.'

With the basic tracks complete, Prince took the tapes to Los Angeles in January 1978, staying in the Hollywood Hills. A further month and a half was spent adding over-dubs at the city's Sound Lab studio. Only when he felt enough work had been done for the day would Prince go sight-seeing, taking photos for a scrapbook he kept. The city's temptations – drinking, casual drug use – so easy for a young musician to find, didn't factor in his lifestyle. 'That would destroy his chances of making it,' Husney said. 'And he wanted to make it.'

In pursuit of perfection, Prince blew his three-album budget, with *For You* costing just $10,000 shy of the $180,000 Warner Bros had fronted as part of their initial deal. Although Mo Ostin and Lenny Waronker raised concerns, Prince brushed them off. 'That would have been like, "Money? What's money? I have to create,"' Marylou Badeaux says, adding, 'He was at the right company to give him that freedom to keep going.'

Prince is credited with playing twenty-seven instruments on *For You* – a variety of synths and keyboards, in the main, as well as guitars, bass, drums and percussion – with the title track alone featuring over forty multi-tracked vocal parts. In setting out to impress, he certainly proved his virtuosity (the local *Saint Paul Dispatch* called the album 'a technical marvel and a curiosity' largely 'because one man did it'), but the weight of overproduction threatened to drag the album down with it.

Its use of synthesizers, however, notably the Oberheim 4-voice, the first in a range of Oberheim models that would define Prince's early recordings, revealed the first flowerings of a pioneering new style of music. Allowing him to eschew arrangements that relied on using real brass instruments, the Oberheim provided a unique sound that filtered the disco/funk template through Prince's vision. 'I created a different kind of horn section by multi-tracking a synthe-sizer and some guitar lines,' he told *The Minneapolis Tribune* in 1978. This innovation – born as much out of financial necessity as it was out of Prince's refusal to be stuck in the past – marked the earliest stages in the development of the 'Minneapolis sound': a synths- and keyboards-driven style of music that would define funk – and much of pop – music in the 1980s.

Warner Bros's promotion teams set about getting *For You* to radio. Although the album leaned more significantly towards R&B than anything else, Russ Thyret insisted his pop department treated Prince as a priority in order to get his music to white audiences. 'They didn't know how to handle it,' Marylou Badeaux recalls. Meanwhile, she worked the R&B stations, some of whom were similarly confused. 'It didn't fit within their conception of what R&B music was,' she says. 'The sound was very different from what he was coming up with. He was streets into the future.'

For You hit No. 21 on *Billboard*'s Soul LPs chart, but stalled at No. 163 on the mainstream Top LPs & Tape chart.

Its lead single, 'Soft and Wet', struggled into the lower reaches of the Hot 100, though a more receptive R&B audience sent it to No. 12 on the Hot Soul Singles chart. Momentum quickly stalled: its follow-up, 'Just As Long As We're Together', limped to No. 91 on the soul chart and didn't even get a showing on the Hot 100.

The album may not have catapulted him to stardom, but it captured a crucial early stage in Prince's development. Largely switching between R&B ballads ('Baby', 'So Blue') and disco-inflected funk ('Soft and Wet', 'Just As Long As We're Together'), with the closing 'I'm Yours' offering a more guitar-driven AOR workout, Prince proved that he could play an array of styles, if not yet synthesize them as he would on later albums. Meanwhile, singing in his trademark falsetto, as he did on most of his early records, helped the kind of subject matter found on 'Soft and Wet' – a Chris Moon co-write relying on a euphemism involving sugarcane – fly under the radar. As Miles Davis observed in his autobiography: 'When he's singing that funky X-rated shit that he does about sex and women … in that girl-like voice he uses, then everyone says it's cute.'

With a view to promoting the album, Prince held signing sessions at record stores around the country. At one event, in Charlotte, North Carolina, three thousand fans rushed the stage, leaving him spooked by their fervour. Not that he was any more comfortable in one-on-one settings with the press. 'He was a terrible interview,' Bob Merlis, Warner Bros's former Senior Vice President Worldwide Corporate Communications, recalls. An early interview found him asking one startled journalist if her pubic hair grew up to her belly button. 'There was a big hue and cry in the office,' Merlis says. 'What are we gonna do with this guy? He'll make more enemies than friends!'

But Prince was 'a shy guy', and interviews were 'the least comfortable thing you could imagine him doing'. 'I can talk about music, but I can't talk about myself,' he told Merlis. 'People ask me these probing questions – I don't know how to answer them.' To Badeaux, he asserted: 'If people would just listen to the music they'd know where my head's at.'

Prince had leased a house at 5215 France Avenue, in Minneapolis's affluent Edina suburb, and expected to take *For You* on tour. Just as Sly Stone had assembled a mixed-race, mixed-sex group for Sly & The Family Stone, Prince's first band as a solo artist helped represent a utopian vision in which gender and race barriers didn't exist, and set the template for what, in the mid-1980s, would become his most famous group: The Revolution. Including white musicians in its line-up also made it harder for the industry to restrict him to the Black market. Now using the surname Cymone, Prince's long-term friend André was back on bass, with Bobby 'Z.' Rivkin on drums. Minneapolis veteran Dez Dickerson joined on guitar, giving the band a punkier edge, and Gayle Chapman and Matt Fink rounded out a double-keyboard line-up.

Despite the group's ideological harmony, external chaos plagued them in these early stages. Rehearsals, initially held at Del's Tire Mart, were moved to cousin Pepé Willie's basement after the band's equipment got stolen. Then Owen Husney quit after Prince began to conflate the responsibilities of a runner – like finding a heater for the basement – with those of a manager trying to take his artist to the next level.

Two showcase gigs at Minneapolis's Capri Theater were booked for January 1979 in order to unveil the new band. Prince's nerves were riding high enough and, yet to develop a stage persona, he struggled to talk to the crowd and sometimes played with his back to the audience – but the second night was particularly fraught.

With Warner Bros representatives in attendance, Prince hoped to convince the label to back a full tour. Dez Dickerson, however, used the show to test out a new wireless pickup – which malfunctioned throughout the night. Unconvinced that he was ready for the road, Warner installed the experienced management team of Bob Cavallo and Joe Ruffalo. A senior employee of Cavallo & Ruffalo, Steve Fargnoli, was dispatched to Minneapolis in the hopes of getting Prince's affairs in order. 'He believed in Prince – a lot,' Roy Bennett, who would soon become Prince's lighting and stage designer, says. 'And he understood what he had as an artist.' Fargnoli would help Prince realize his greatest successes throughout the decade that followed.

* * * * *

For You ended in a bust, but Prince learned from his mistakes. 'I knew how to make hits by my second album,' he later told *Rolling Stone*. Engineer Susan Rogers, who at this point was just an early fan, agrees: 'That first record was craft-heavy … His original ideas broke through on the next record. You can hear on the *Prince* album: this kid can write.'

Prince spent just a couple of months in Burbank's Alpha Studios in order to prove exactly that. Released on 19 October 1979, the *Prince* album hit No. 22 on the Top LPs & Tape chart – one hundred and forty-one places higher than its predecessor – while climbing to No. 3 on the soul chart. It boasted no fewer than three signature Prince cuts: 'I Wanna Be Your Lover' (No. 11 on the Hot 100; No. 1 on the Hot Soul Singles chart), 'Why You Wanna Treat Me So Bad?' (No. 13 soul) and 'Sexy Dancer', whose near-nine-minute 12-inch mix received so much airplay that DJs sent it to the Top 5 of *Billboard*'s Disco 100.

Dispensing with the charade of an external producer – executive or otherwise – Prince was aided by engineer Gary Brandt, who helped him concoct a tighter, more stripped-down sound. With a less laboured production and fewer overdubs, Prince made every element count: 'I Wanna Be Your Lover' wove musical elements in and out – guitar licks, keyboard stabs – in order to keep the groove fresh. Anchored by power chords, driven by catchy keyboard runs and including Prince's first guitar solo of note, 'Why You Wanna Treat Me So Bad?' took rock music to the dancefloor, while the all-out rock track 'Bambi' saw him flirting openly with sexual taboos for the first time, delivering a message to a lesbian love interest: sex would be better with him.

Sung in 'the most thrilling R&B falsetto since Smokey Robinson', in *Rolling Stone*'s estimation, Prince may have made 'Bambi''s more outré lyrics palatable, but the track's sonic aggression would have left no doubt as to his true intentions. Compared to *For You*, the *Prince* album went up a gear: the funky songs are funkier; the ballads less mawkish.

After drilling his band throughout the year, Prince buried any memories of the Capri Theater shows with another industry showcase, this time at Leeds Instrument Rentals, in Los Angeles, in November 1979, where he proved to Warner Bros that he had what it took to command a stage. ('I couldn't even sleep that night,' Marylou Badeaux recalls. 'I said, "Oh my god. I think we just saw the second coming."')

Hitting the road in support of his new album, Prince toured through to May 1980, including a 16 December appearance on Dick Clark's *American Bandstand* for his first national television performance. Like Ed Sullivan before him, and Simon Cowell's *X Factor* in later decades, Dick Clark guaranteed exposure in millions of households. Although his viewing figures were on the decline by the end of the 1970s, as a symbol of white, middle-class acceptability, Clark could still make or break an artist. When Prince, uncomfortable in front of TV cameras for the first time and annoyed at the host's assertion that 'this is not the kind of music that comes from Minneapolis' ('That really gave me an attitude for the rest of the talk,' he told *Star Tribune* reporter Jon Bream), offered just hand gestures and mumbled responses to Clark's questions, his bandmates thought he was sabotaging the opportunity.

Even more shocking was Prince's appearance. Clad entirely in gold – high heels, open shirt and spandex that left little to the imagination – he performed two songs, with his band looking like extras from the 1979 New York gang romp *The Warriors* (Matt Fink standing out in a prison jumpsuit). But it was a relatively demure outfit given what Prince would soon wear on stage. Arguing with his managers over his refusal to wear underwear beneath the spandex, he resolved the problem by taking them at their literal word: ditching the leggings, he began appearing on stage in ladies' bikini briefs. 'I wear what I wear because I don't like clothes,' Prince asserted. 'It's what's comfortable.'

Writing in his memoir *The Confessions of Rick James: Memoirs of a Super Freak*, the Motown star described 'this little dude wearing high heels, standing there in a trench coat' with 'little girl's bloomers' underneath, in a disparaging entry that overlooks one important aspect: Prince, who had been hired to support James on his 1980 *Fire It Up* tour, kicked the headliner's ass. 'Rick wasn't a very nice person,' Roy Bennett recalls of the acrimonious tour, during which James began putting restrictions on them, interfering with their production. 'I think he felt pressure from Prince.' Prince, meanwhile, felt that the headliner wasn't even in his league. Gaining confidence each night, he found it amusing that he could antagonize James so easily. 'It was sport for him,' Bennett says.

Having won over James's audience on stage, the next step was to beat the self-proclaimed inventor of punk-funk on record. Immediately after finishing the tour, Prince retreated to his home studio, in a newly rented property at 680 North Arm Drive, in Orono, Minnesota, to work on his third album. Recorded in even less time than its predecessor, *Dirty Mind* came as a shock – in more ways than one. Fittingly, for an album recorded at home, it drew as much on the DIY ethic of the late 1970s and early 1980s punk and new wave movements as it did on the R&B and funk palette of his first two records.

This creative synthesis saw Prince merge traditionally Black and white music in a way no one had ever attempted before, seeking to broaden his audience in the process. Warner Bros, however, didn't know how to receive it: with songs like 'When You Were Mine', a catchy piece of power-pop that came to Prince while he was listening to John Lennon, their new Stevie Wonder suddenly sounded like The Cars. And these recordings were raw, nowhere near the polished sound that would attract mainstream airplay.

Even more concerning was the album's lyrical content. Dispensing with the euphemisms and sly come-ons, *Dirty Mind* was as brazen as its title suggested, with songs that celebrated oral sex and incest sitting alongside others that found Prince unable – or unwilling – to hide his urges any longer. 'A couple of people higher up tried to suggest to him that he might want to tone it down a bit,' Marylou Badeaux recalls. 'He wanted to push buttons ... He found it damned funny that people would get all riled up about these things.'

When he did dial back on carnal affairs, the songs were no less hedonistic, celebrating lifestyles in which people did whatever they wanted in the pursuit of thrills. Album closer 'Partyup' included an anti-war chant that expressed a political worldview that, like his sexual one, demanded freedom of choice.

For Prince, *Dirty Mind* 'really felt like me for once'. It hit the shelves on 8 October 1980 and went out to radio stations with a stickered warning for DJs – audition before airing. The cover, however, was alarming enough: Prince described his aggressively androgynous look as one of 'pure sexuality'; everyone else saw a stark black-and-white image of the musician standing before upturned bed springs, dressed in a trench coat studded on one shoulder, bikini briefs, a neckerchief and a 2-Tone 'Rude Boy' badge underscoring the message. The rear sleeve found him lying on a bed, stocking-clad legs splayed, beneath a spray-painted tracklist dripping like the residue from a sordid reverie.

As bold a creative leap as *Dirty Mind* was, not everyone wanted to be involved. Keyboardist Gayle Chapman, increasingly uncomfortable with some of the acts she had been asked to simulate on stage, had left the group at the end of the previous tour, while band rehearsals took on a different tone when Prince's dad dropped by. 'Don't cuss,' Prince would tell them. 'Don't say any of the bad words. Just play the music.'

Dirty Mind's inner sleeve revealed his new line-up posing in front of a brick wall, their names graffitied above them: Lisa Coleman had replaced the departing keyboardist, while cheap suits, flasher macs and bare chests were the unofficial uniform for all except Matt 'Dr.' Fink, whose medical scrubs and stethoscope would identify him from here on out. The group seemed to offer unity for misfit individuals who struggled to find their place in society. 'The word "alternative" was something he used for a long time before it actually became a musical category,' Coleman says. 'We felt like we would be an alternative for people who didn't fit in anywhere else.'

It was this line-up that took *Dirty Mind* on tour in December, with practical jokes becoming another part of Prince's repertoire. 'He would just really mess with people's heads. He had kind of an awkward sense of humour,'

Roy Bennett says. A favourite gag was to sit in a wheelchair in the airport, with his sunglasses on, before falling onto the floor to get a reaction from passers-by. 'We wanted to shock people and just get attention,' says Coleman, whose stage attire would sometimes amount to 'just a bra and some jeans'. 'Even if it was bad attention – it didn't matter … It was just like: everybody be outrageous.'

Meanwhile, Prince continued to build a fanbase in strongholds like Detroit, where, thanks to the efforts of local promoter Billy Sparks and radio DJ The Electrifying Mojo, he had earned a loyal following from the beginning. With its musical history rooted in Motown, and its own new sound – techno – on the horizon, the city was perfectly primed to embrace a rising star that straddled both classic soul and a new electronic future of music. But Prince struggled to get over in outposts like Chattanooga, Tennessee.

'Unfortunately, those markets being so conservative … they couldn't wrap their heads around this little skinny guy in leg warmers and a trench coat and bikini briefs,' Roy Bennett says. With ticket and album sales failing to match the music's artistic ambitions, the tour was put on hold while a newly hired publicist, Howard Bloom, went to work drumming up support from the media.

'Will the Little Girls Understand?' asked the headline of a *Rolling Stone* feature that kick-started a press scramble to acknowledge Prince's brilliance. Awarding *Dirty Mind* four and a half stars out of five, the same magazine proclaimed it 'the most generous album about sex ever made by a man'. The buzz crossed the Atlantic to the UK, whose *NME* observed: 'Prince refuses to play it safe. If he did, he wouldn't have made this album.'

The tour was back on, the group playing in smaller club venues, but selling them out. 'The hype was so big,' Bennett recalls, 'the amount of people that would show up, and the excitement of showing up in town, it was really building.' Although *Dirty Mind* fell short of *Prince*'s commercial success – it peaked at No. 45 in the mainstream chart and No. 7 in the soul chart – it received the critical praise Prince needed at the end of his initial three-album deal with Warner Bros.

Rolling Stone may have called him 'the unlikeliest rock star, Black or white, in recent memory', but *Dirty Mind* was the first step in an artistic trajectory unparalleled in popular music. 'He showed that he understood how the game is played,' Susan Rogers notes. 'The tactic of doing a third album that was aimed almost exclusively at music critics … When you do that, they'll write about you. And when they write about you, they will help you achieve fame.' The reinvention that took him there shocked everybody, but for Prince there was no cause for surprise: 'I wasn't being deliberately provocative,' he asserted. 'I was being deliberately me.'

3

Apocalypse Wow

After releasing *Dirty Mind*, Prince realized he could 'get away with anything I want to get away with. All I have to do is be myself.' Being himself, however, came with complications: there were so many facets of his personality, it was impossible to channel them into just one persona. Meanwhile, his creativity was developing at such a rate that the usual business model – release an album, tour it; release an album, tour it – was, like the limitations of the recording process itself, unable to keep up. Minneapolis, too, could be restrictive: the city 'basically got all the new music and dances three months late', he told *Rolling Stone*. The remedy was to 'do my own thing. Otherwise, when we did split Minneapolis, we were gonna be way behind and dated.'

Inspired by the 1980 movie *The Idolmaker*, in which a rock manager masterminds the careers of two teen stars, Prince decided he would become a Svengali himself, developing local talent that would make it seem as though he were spearheading a new movement emerging from his hometown. 'He was determined to have it appear that there was a scene,' Susan Rogers says. 'There was no one else who was doing exactly what he was doing … The belief among the general public that there was a scene happening in

Minneapolis served his ends better than the belief that there's this one guy and he's this mega genius.'

'The more he started realizing who he was, the more he realized some of the stuff he writes doesn't fit in that lane,' Lisa Coleman says. 'So: "What do I do with these things that I write when I feel kind of goofy? Or when I feel kind of feminine?" He just had a range and an ability to express himself in all these different ways.'

Shortly after recording his self-titled second album, Prince had made an initial attempt at developing a roster he could control. A brief stint with singer Sue Ann Carwell came to nothing. A short-lived project with his backing band – The Rebels, which focused on rockier material than Prince was releasing under his own name – was devised in order to keep them busy during downtime, so they wouldn't leave in pursuit of other work, as much as it was the collaborative affair he presented it as. An album's worth of material was recorded in Boulder, Colorado, before being quickly forgotten. His next side project, however, would outgrow even Prince's expectations and, at times, come to challenge his own popularity.

School friend and former Grand Central drummer Morris Day remained part of Prince's entourage. Acting as a runner and filming concerts for Prince to critique later in the evenings, he also kept his hand in on the drums, playing with local groups; it had been a Morris Day groove that inspired *Dirty Mind*'s closing track, 'Partyup'. In return for its use, Prince made Day an offer: $10,000 or help forming his own band. Choosing the latter, Day found himself fronting The Time.

Picking band members from Grand Central's rivals, Prince assembled a group of versatile musicians who could perform live the songs he recorded for them in the studio: keyboardist Jimmy 'Jam' Harris and bassist Terry Lewis – later to become 1980s and 1990s hitmakers in their own right – synth player Monte Moir, guitarist Jesse Johnson and drummer Garry 'Jellybean' Johnson, with dancer/comic foil Jerome Benton completing the line-up. But while the musicians posed for their self-titled debut album's front cover – dressed in retro suits and thin ties, like a new wave update on the fashions favoured by Prince's father – and would come to tear it up night after night on stage, only Morris's singing and playing would actually feature on the record, alongside a few performances from Prince's own keyboardists, Lisa Coleman and Matt Fink.

Following Prince's guide vocals, Day sang the funky, upbeat numbers that Prince wrote and performed while channelling his emerging Jamie Starr alter ego. Credited as an engineer on *Dirty Mind*, Starr was a brash and moneyed fast-talker, a self-styled ladies' man not lacking in confidence. 'He would even dress up like Jamie Starr,' Lisa Coleman says. 'It wasn't just a pen name … He would just be these different people. It was remarkable.'

The character also provided Day with the template for his own frontman act. Through The Time, Prince explored other avenues of expression, making music that referenced that Black idioms and preferences he had grown up with but which didn't fit the persona he had created for his own albums. 'The Time represented a kind of Black culture that was more pure and more distilled than Prince's own cultural make-up,' Susan Rogers says. 'Prince lived in, worked in and expressed white culture as well as he did Black culture, and had the musicality of The Time been incorporated into Prince … he would have been less successful.' Realizing this, Prince was 'clever enough to parse them out under two different umbrellas'.

Signature early Time songs such as 'Get It Up' and 'Cool' became hit singles on the soul chart, while their debut album hit No. 7 soul and even cracked the mainstream Top 50. With the group providing an outlet for the kind of funk and R&B music that would keep Prince's original audience happy, he could focus on expanding his sound further with *Dirty Mind*'s follow-up, *Controversy*.

Playing his first overseas gigs – Amsterdam, London and Paris – at the end of spring 1981, Prince encountered the UK's New Romantic scene and the electronica music then pervading the European clubs – mechanical, sometimes glacial, songs by the likes of Gary Numan and Kraftwerk. Back home, in the studio basement installed in his recently purchased two-storey house on Chanhassen's Kiowa Trail, where the purple-painted building backed on to Lake Riley, and throughout recording sessions that continued at Hollywood Sound Recorders and his favoured Sunset Sound, in Los Angeles, Prince assimilated these styles into his own new wave/funk hybrid.

The home studio felt like 'a secret laboratory', Coleman says. 'We were in Prince's lair and we could create these things sort of in a vacuum … It became more potent. It was like Prince concentrate.'

The resulting album, from its artwork through to its music, pushed the *Dirty Mind* aesthetic forward.

A full-colour, fully clothed Prince – studded purple trench coat, waistcoat, shirt and necktie – stared from the album cover before a backdrop of copies of the fictional *Controversy Daily*, whose socio-political headlines ('Do You Believe in God', 'President Signs Gun Control Act'), hinted that *Controversy*, which was released on 14 October 1981, less than three months after *The Time*, would do more than upend sexual mores.

If its title track toyed with some of the media's own confused response to Prince – was he Black? White? Straight? Gay? Did he fulfil your expectations? – and left some listeners mishearing the title as 'I want your pussy', it also threw in a recitation of the Lord's Prayer alongside a rejection of clothing, racial barriers and rules. 'A lot of the band was religious in different ways,' says Coleman, not a believer herself. 'It had different meanings to all of us to say the Lord's Prayer in the middle of the song. To me it was more like an art piece. You've never quite heard the Lord's Prayer like that.'

As a declaration of intent, it framed the album perfectly: here was a statement on sex and politics at the start of the new decade. 'Let's Work', 'Jack U Off' and 'Do Me, Baby' were among those songs that furthered Prince's quest for sexual liberation (he would return to 'Do Me, Baby' throughout his career, singling it out in his memoir as a song that 'took the R&B ballad form' of the 1970s and 'updated it for the eighties'); 'Ronnie, Talk to Russia' and 'Annie Christian' revealed an increasing concern over the state of the world – Cold War paranoia, gun crime; the assassination of John Lennon, the deaths of Black children.

'More than my songs have to do with sex, they have to do with one human's love for one another, which goes deeper than anything political that anybody could possibly write about,' Prince had told the UK's *Melody Maker* earlier that year. But he also worried that 'these things don't necessarily come out', acknowledging, 'my attitude's so sexual that it overshadows anything else'.

As an artistic statement, *Controversy* didn't have *Dirty Mind*'s clarity, but it did see Prince working towards unifying his subject matter in the same way that he would his musical influences. If at least one publication, Minneapolis's *Sweet Potato*, suggested that *Controversy* may have made more sense if it were split into 'a serious side and a sex side', it also noted that separating the two would be an easier task 'if the penis weren't a political tool in Prince's worldview'.

The singles 'Controversy' and 'Let's Work' still performed far better in the R&B market than the mainstream one, but *Controversy*'s overall sales improved significantly on *Dirty Mind*'s, with the album peaking at No. 21 on *Billboard*'s Top LPs & Tape chart and hitting No. 3 soul. 'It was right on the edge, and I could feel his managers were really excited because it seemed like either this album was going to break it or the next one was going to,' Coleman says. Yet mainstream acceptance was still some way off, as a humiliating experience would make all too obvious.

Preparing for his own headlining tour, Prince was booked to open for The Rolling Stones at LA's Memorial Coliseum on 9 and 11 October. First on the bill before the more straightforward rock fare of George Thorogood & The Destroyers and The J. Geils Band, Prince's androgynous look and the open sexuality of his songs provoked the Stones' audience into booing and pelting the band with whatever they could lay their hands on.

'It was so bizarre, because Mick was totally androgynous,' Roy Bennett says, 'but that crowd' – drunken revellers with a prevalent biker mentality – 'completely overlooked that part of him … It was heartbreaking watching Prince get stuff thrown at him and booed.'

His ego 'completely annihilated', Prince quit the stage several songs into his set, took a car straight to the airport and flew back to Minneapolis, refusing to play the second night's show. 'There was no stopping him,' Bennett says. 'It was like, boom, and he was home.' It took everybody to convince him to come back, manager Steve Fargnoli, guitarist Dez Dickerson and Mick Jagger – himself a fan, and the Stone who had made the support-slot recommendation – included.

Before Prince's appearance on the second night, tour promoter Bill Graham called the audience 'a bunch of fucking assholes', promising them, 'You'll be spending a lot of money to come see this guy in a couple of years.' That didn't discourage them from carrying out their planned bombardment – a bag of rotting chicken, a full bottle of Jack Daniel's, a gallon jug of orange juice. 'It was probably worse because people came prepared,' Lisa Coleman says. 'But the fact that he came back and did it a second time is really something to be proud of … We were like, "Fuck that." We shortened our set and played the more rock tunes – not so much funk or anything that would scare the white people.' It was the final time Prince performed a support slot.

The experience was a baptism of fire for Prince's new bassist, Mark Brown, a former 7-Eleven employee who, rechristened BrownMark, had replaced André Cymone in the group. (Increasingly frustrated at his sideman role, and feeling that Prince had taken to stealing his ideas – including the basic parts for 'Do Me, Baby' – Cymone had decided it was time to focus on his own music.)

But Prince's experience at the hands of the Stones' fans didn't inspire him to take care of his own support act on the *Controversy* tour, which launched on 20 November. Animosity between Prince and The Time grew throughout the four months they spent on the road together, partly fuelled by The Time's determination to put on a show that would make up for their no-show on their own album, and partly fuelled by Prince's growing aloofness, exacerbated by his latest hire, personal bodyguard Charles 'Big Chick' Huntsberry. 'I think he felt like he needed some kind of security blanket,' Roy Bennett says. 'He started to see his vulnerability. He had issues from growing up ... obviously he was very self-conscious about his height and a lot of things ... It was the beginning of an insulation.'

Matching the ambition of the *Controversy* material, Prince's stage design was a tiered set with ramps, a catwalk, a fireman's pole and Venetian blinds, conceived by Roy Bennett, whose initial concept – instrument risers and microphone stands inspired by the female forms that made for the Korova Milkbar's furniture in Stanley Kubrick's film *A Clockwork Orange*; projections of 'basically orgies' onto the audience, 'so the band had something to watch' – was nixed by a rising artist wary of attracting the wrong kind of attention. 'He loved the idea, but he was scared of the women's rights movement,' Bennett recalls. 'He knew we'd get slammed.' Instead, they opted for moody lighting and shadows that created a sense of mystery. 'During the 1980s, Venetian blinds was a very suggestive, sexual image,' Bennett says. 'It was about what you couldn't see.'

By contrast, The Time just had their music. Improving night after night, their taut funk, aided by Morris Day's evolving stage presence and Jerome Benton's comic turns – presenting Day with a mirror, so he could check his appearance mid-song – was easier for some audiences to digest than the more cerebral concepts Prince had introduced into his live shows.

'He created something that he was fighting against,' Bennett says. 'Because they were a monster band. They kicked his ass every night.' Fearing that he would be upstaged – as he himself had upstaged Rick James just a year before – Prince began dropping the group from the bill. 'The tension between the two – they were competing against each other,' Bennett says. 'The audience fucking benefited from that whole thing in a big way.'

But there was 'a dark side' that 'got out of control a couple of times'. On the tour's final night, at Cincinnati Riverfront Coliseum, on 14 March 1982, the animosity spilled over into a physical confrontation: from the side of the stage, Prince and his band threw eggs at The Time; after their set, Jesse Johnson was handcuffed to a wall-mounted coat rack while Prince continued his onslaught. 'It got really ugly,' Bennett says. 'If he could have, he would have ripped the pole out.'

The Time were ordered not to retaliate during Prince's headlining slot, but as soon as he left the stage a food fight erupted, developing into a real fight at the hotel: punches were thrown amid more food and insults. At the end of the evening, already aggrieved at receiving what he felt was an unfair salary for his band, Morris, accused of starting the ordeal, was handed the cleaning bill.

* * * * *

Barely pausing to survey the damage – not only to the hotel, but to his relationship with The Time – Prince was back in the studio, again expanding both his sound and his roster. If his androgynous look was an external expression of the male and female impulses that coexisted within him, Prince now envisioned a girl group through which to channel the feminine aspect of his psyche. His initial concept – The Hookers – was quickly reconceptualized when he met Denise Matthews backstage at the 1982 American Music Awards. A furious Rick James, losing out again, watched as sparks flew between his rival and his date: with her feline eyes and a complexion similar to Prince's, she was said to have appeared to him as a female version of himself. ('He really fell in love with her,' Lisa Coleman says.) As Matthews once told the story, Prince invited her to the bathroom so he could try her coat on; when he removed his own leopard-print coat, he had nothing on underneath.

That was, effectively, the costume design for Vanity 6, the group that Matthews, renamed Vanity (after nixing Prince's original choice: Vagina, pronounced 'Vageena'), fronted as his latest protégé, making for an awkward situation in which she was promoted to both group leader and top billing in Prince's growing list of girlfriends. 'He and I would have terrible arguments' about the clothing, says Brenda Bennett, wife of set designer Roy, who had originally been enlisted to help with wardrobe and to film shows on the *Controversy* tour, and now, along with Susan Moonsie, one of Prince's longer-standing girlfriends, flanked Vanity in the group. 'There's a difference between trashy lingerie and tasteful, classy lingerie.'

Prince pushed for trashy before finally reaching a compromise. With André Cymone's mother, Bernadette, sometimes making their costumes, Brenda would be the 'punk' of the group and Susan 'the sexy little girl with the teddy bear'. Vanity, meanwhile, channelled her 'raw animal magnetism … she just ripped it up'. Despite not having any experience as a singer, Vanity's sultry attitude was perfect for songs like 'Nasty Girl', 'Wet Dream' and 'Drive Me Wild'.

With Brenda having performed throughout the 1970s with The Tombstone Blues Band, Prince relied on her to 'keep this shit together' like a den mother. Envisioned as his take on The Supremes, and in part the embodiment of a male fantasy (The Time were 'for the girls, and he wanted to have something for the guys'), Vanity 6 gave him yet another persona to write for. 'He wasn't so male that he couldn't open up the female side of things in terms of trying to look at something with a woman's eyes,' Brenda says.

In turn, two years before Madonna released 'Like a Virgin', Vanity 6 'opened up things for other female bands that came after us – the whole sexuality thing, if nothing else. That was a turning point for music.' More new wave than The Time's elastic funk, the *Vanity 6* album, released on 11 August 1982, nevertheless made No. 6 on *Billboard*'s Black LPs chart (and No. 45 in the mainstream chart), with 'Nasty Girl' hitting No. 7 on the Black Singles chart and topping the Dance/Disco Top 80.

'In Prince's world, things moved so quickly that even vicious fights could be forgotten in a flash,' Morris Day would later recall in his memoir, *On Time: A Princely Life in Funk*. 'We wanted to ride his rocket ship to the moon.' Enticed by a pay rise and another opportunity to build their own fanbase while supporting Prince on tour, The Time stood by while Prince recorded their second album, *What Time is It?* Released just two weeks after *Vanity 6*, it effectively picked up from where their debut album left off, with 'Wild and Loose', '777-9311' (named after Dez Dickerson's phone number – a move that forced the guitarist to find a new one when fans started calling) and 'Gigolos Get Lonely Too' furthering the Morris Day persona even as Prince, once again, took control in the studio.

Improving on its predecessor's chart performance (it hit No. 6 on the Top LPs & Tape and No. 2 on the Black LPs charts, respectively), *What Time is It?* proved that The Time had attracted a following. In creating a cadre of local groups to surround him, Prince – or Jamie Starr, the nominal mastermind behind both new albums – had succeeded in making his hometown the focal point for a musical movement. While some, like the UK's *Melody Maker*, thought The Time and Vanity 6 were plagiarists, and

Prince himself publicly maintained his distance ('I'm not Jamie Starr,' he asserted to the *Los Angeles Times*), others realized that the groups were part of a cultural shift driven by one man hitting a creative peak – and whose prolific work rate saw him not only conceptualizing multiple projects simultaneously, but creating a wealth of surplus material that wouldn't even be released.

While working on songs for his side projects, Prince also recorded the album that would give him true mainstream success, splitting his time between his home studio and Sunset Sound. Fuelled by Styrofoam cups of coffee three-quarters full with sugar cubes, and a diet of Toblerone and Doritos, he would write, record and mix entire songs in twenty-four-hour stints, with only engineer Peggy McCreary, who had previously worked with him at the end of the *Controversy* sessions, for company.

'He told me one time that the only reason he went home was so I could sleep,' McCreary says. 'Because he didn't need to sleep.' If she tried to feed him, he would accuse her of trying to make him tired ('No, I'm just kind of hungry'); years later, when he switched to drinking Earl Grey tea, engineers would staple the labels on to decaf bags in order to try and reduce his caffeine intake. Needing to be 'at his beck and call, no matter what time of day or night it was', McCreary ended up quitting smoking to avoid the hassle of leaving the room; 'out of necessity', she taught him how to punch in his own vocals so that she could put her feet up for a few minutes. Eventually, during the half-decade they worked together, Prince ordered a bed for the studio. 'It wasn't for what everybody was tittering about,' McCreary says. 'It was for me to take a nap.'

But with Prince's reputation, Sunset Sound's receptionist had initially tried to dissuade McCreary from working with him on her own. 'He writes really dirty songs about giving head and stuff,' she warned of the guy who never attended sessions in less than full regalia – suited, hair done, six-inch-high heels marking a distinctive walk that indicated what kind of mood he would be in that day – but whose tambourines and plectrums were printed with the directive 'Love God'.

McCreary was surprised when she met him: 'He was shy and quiet, and I was kind of taken aback by how withdrawn he was … There was a very sexual side that would come out in his music, but his actual persona was very respectful.'

Juggling the Vanity 6, The Time and Prince albums, McCreary sometimes wasn't sure what they were working on: 'You just had to facilitate his creative energy, which was all over the place all the time. And he never wanted to hear "No". He never wanted anything to break down.' In Minneapolis, after leading the groups through rehearsals, he would record in his home studio, capturing more ideas, among them his new album's eventual title track. Allegedly recorded last of all, after Warner Bros felt the record needed a 'Dirty Mind' or a 'Controversy' – a song to provide a thematic marker for the whole project – Prince sandwiched its creation between a late-night rehearsal with The Time and a follow-up session the next day.

'1999' not only provided the *1999* album with its jumping-off point, it drew the disparate threads of Prince's earlier albums into one unifying whole: we're fucked; let's fuck. He then ran this celebration of abandonment in the face of death through different iterations – neon-lit nocturnal ballad ('Little Red Corvette'), taut electro-funk ('D.M.S.R.') and S&M fever dream ('Automatic') – creating his first truly seamless artistic statement.

If *Controversy* struggled to find a balance between sex and politics, the new wave overdrive of 'Let's Pretend We're Married' merged these dualities with ease, its sexual forthrightness sitting next to an exhortation to God as if they were natural bedfellows. It was the most successful to date of Prince's attempts to resolve his sexual and religious urges. But for all the album's explicit subject matter, its creator understood the ambiguities of sexual politics better than anything – or anyone – else. Sometimes vulnerable, other times assertive, on *1999* he largely exists somewhere between the two, reconciling contradictions and seeking new ways of dissolving boundaries.

'I see New York a little bit more,' Prince told *Musician* in 1983. 'In my subconscious I'm influenced by the sinisterness of it, you know, the power. I hear sirens all the time, things like that.' There's a claustrophobic, urban feel to *1999*; sirens, calls for police help and other indicators of inner-city distress are woven into the album, heightening its apocalyptic paranoia. But *1999*'s defining sound came from Prince's unique mastery of the latest studio technology: 'There's nothing like the feeling after you've done something and play it back, and you know that you'll never hear anything like it and that they'll never figure it out,' he said after finishing the record.

One of the album's sonic trademarks is the Linn LM-1 drum machine. First used on *Controversy*'s 'Private Joy', this new piece of recording technology underpinned almost every track on *1999*, providing a solid anchor for Prince's increasingly complex synthesizer arrangements. 'I was always amazed at how he could manipulate that Linn drum,' Peggy McCreary says. 'He programmed that thing better than anybody I've ever seen.' Layering guitars and keyboards on top, he perfected the 'Minneapolis sound', spawning a decade's worth of imitators in the process.

Hitting the shelves on 27 October 1982, *1999* was so precise in its vision and engaging in its inventiveness that, despite running to seventy minutes, it never felt overlong. Warner Bros, however, had to be convinced to release it as a 'specially-priced two record set' – a double album, for the price of a single – in order to retain Prince's artistic integrity without alienating potential buyers. (In Europe, it was shorn to seven tracks and issued as a single album, before being reissued in full in 1983.)

Storming *Billboard*'s Black Singles and Dance/Disco charts (hitting No. 4 and No. 1, respectively), '1999' initially fell short of Prince's mainstream ambitions, peaking at No. 44 on the Hot 100. Its promo video, however, found him capturing the zeitgeist and – finally – the attention of MTV. 'We'd made videos for years, on all the albums,' says Lisa Coleman. 'They didn't get much play because MTV was just pretty much a hair-band channel – heavy rock – and we didn't quite fit in.'

Debuting in December, the '1999' clip made Prince the first Black artist to appear on the nascent cable TV channel. 'He opened up the rock marketplace for Black performers,' Bob Merlis says. 'The idea of Black performers being accepted by a white audience – that had a huge impact on integration and the cause of civil rights.' Essentially updating Prince's previous promo videos with a bigger budget, slicker performances and sharper editing, the '1999' clip also offered a glimpse of what were fast becoming the most talked-about live shows on the planet, introducing mainstream America to the Prince world: boldly conceived, uniquely stylized, highly oversexed. (Having been asked to sing backing vocals on the song, a platinum-blonde Jill Jones, also sharing space with Susan Moonsie and Vanity in Prince's bed, made for a notable presence alongside Lisa Coleman.)

'The basis of what we were doing was creating this very sensual, sexual world of intrigue,' Roy Bennett says. Like a cross between the sci-fi film noir of *Blade Runner* and the yet-to-be-released erotic thriller *9½ Weeks*, the smoky, red-and-purple-drenched sets made the most of Bennett's Venetian blinds, while Prince's purple lamé trench coat signified his evolution from the punk aesthetic. In the wake of David Bowie's ground-breaking 'Ashes to Ashes' video, the '1999' clip pointed the way for other iconic promos to come, such as Eurythmics's 'Sweet Dreams (Are Made of This)' and Michael Jackson's 'Beat It', revealing Prince's understanding of the format: a memorable clip wasn't just about capturing a great performance, it was about creating performance art.

Further videos – 'Little Red Corvette', 'Let's Pretend We're Married' and 'Automatic' – expanded upon the scene-setting of '1999', helping to send a reissue of the title track to No. 12 and 'Little Red Corvette' to No. 6 on the Hot 100 chart, and propelling their parent album into the

Top 10. Prince had finally become the crossover star he had always claimed to be: musically diverse, appealing to Black and white audiences, breaking down barriers to acceptance.

With this as a backdrop, he set out on the *1999* tour (also dubbed *The Triple Threat* tour), which ran from November 1982 through to April 1983. Expanding on the *Controversy* stage design, Prince brought a brass bed on the road for a set piece that would see him open the diagonal flap of his trousers, appearing to expose himself in silhouette. With Vanity 6 and The Time as support acts, 'It was Prince's Travelling Medicine Show,' Roy Bennett says. 'And it was building this empire.'

While outwardly successful, internally the Prince camp was once again in disarray. Travelling together on a bus, Vanity, Jill Jones and Susan Moonsie were left to deal with each other – and the knowledge of 'ancillary' women who would catch Prince's eye at shows – wondering which of them would get to spend the night with him. 'It was pretty brutal,' Bennett says. 'You've got three girls all in love with him … I think there was a side of it that he felt was fun tension … I don't know that he ever actually thought about how harmful it was.'

'He always had this extremely strong, unexplainable aura,' Marylou Badeaux notes. 'He got women to where they were just absolutely so head over heels in love with him – he could not return that.' But while 'on a business level, he had a very, very strong respect for women', including Peggy McCreary, Susan Rogers, Lisa Coleman, future guitarist Wendy Melvoin and Badeaux herself, 'when it came to the personal side of things', Badeaux says, 'He never had the tools to understand how to treat a woman … And that comes from how he was brought up.'

The Time, too, continued to feel mistreated, finding themselves dropped from the bill at major stops like New York and Los Angeles. 'Management was starting to feel like we shouldn't have a funky band play before us … it wasn't necessarily a great pairing, business-wise,' Lisa Coleman says. Although feeling as though they 'were part of the same family', Prince 'had to accept that not only could he not support anybody, but if he was going to have a support band, it had to be the right thing and not just all Prince bands'.

Compounding their resentment, The Time were also required to play back-up to Vanity 6 while hidden behind a curtain. 'Our show was so short that we were actually doing them a favour,' Brenda Bennett asserts: they got to have a fifteen-minute warm-up before their own set. But Morris Day, who was getting more involved with cocaine, didn't see it that way. 'It was influencing his ego and how he wanted to do things. And he wanted to have more control.'

Looking to make some money on the side, keyboardist Jimmy Jam and bassist Terry Lewis set themselves up as a production duo. After overseeing a session for The S.O.S. Band, they found themselves snowed in at Atlanta, Georgia, missing a show in San Antonio.

'Prince was fucking livid,' says Lisa Coleman, who stood in for Jam, playing offstage with Prince, who performed Lewis's bass parts while Jerome Benton mimed in front of the audience.

'Prince was very possessive,' Roy Bennett says. 'How he was with women, he was with his artists … So for Terry and Jimmy to leave the bubble was a slap in the face to him. And he never forgave them for that.' Prince fined the duo upon their return. At the end of the tour he sacked them – or, rather, forced Morris Day to sack them, undermining Day's leadership of his own group.

The *1999* tour almost imploded. As a married couple, Roy and Brenda assumed parental roles, keeping stress levels 'down to a dull roar'. Alan Leeds, a former James Brown tour manager, was brought in to prevent disaster, initially communicating through Prince's bodyguard, Big Chick, while earning Prince's trust. Meanwhile, casualties piled up: Vanity developed alcohol and drug dependencies that would grow to alarming proportions in the following years; even Dez Dickerson was ready to throw in the towel.

'He was really out of sorts with the whole thing – with what was going on behind the lyrics,' Brenda Bennett says. 'And he was working on his own stuff.' But those who remained felt they were heading towards something big. Soon to join Prince in his marathon stints in the studio – giving a relieved Peggy McCreary some camaraderie – Susan Rogers recalls: 'For the cognoscenti, he was the right artist for the right time. And *that* is such a vital foundation for a long career.'

4

Purple Reign

lthough, artistically, Prince always looked to the future, he also fastidiously archived his past. As his fame grew in the 1980s, and the truly prolific nature of his output became clearer, stories spread about a vault – 'The Vault' – harbouring a lifetime's worth of material, both released and unreleased, which, over decades, amounted to an overwhelming record of his prodigious creativity. An increasing number of live performances stacked up alongside studio recordings; among these were staged dramatic scenes and *Controversy* tour footage for a project entitled *The Second Coming*.

The film was scrapped before completion, but Prince, who had long been fascinated by cinema, still harboured ambitions to create a full-length movie. By the end of the *1999* tour, he'd worked up a treatment for a semi-autobiographical film. With his contract with Cavallo, Ruffalo & Fargnoli up for renegotiation, Prince gave the team an ultimatum: he wanted to star in the movie, he wanted his name above the title, and he wanted it to be at a major studio. If they failed to secure the deal, they'd lose their fastest-rising client.

'There was no precedent for this,' observed Alan Leeds, who had begun to oversee the daily running of Prince's growing empire. 'Rock'n'roll stars with a couple of hit albums did not make major movies. Let alone someone from the Black community having the gumption to do it in the mainstream.'

Warner Bros's filmmaking arm, Warner Bros Pictures, felt the same way and hesitated to finance a project that carried such risk. Backing Prince, however, was Warner Bros Records's exec Mo Ostin, who invested $4 million to get production underway. 'We felt we were on the edge – just on the cusp of something beyond,' Marylou Badeaux says.

An eleven-page treatment, handwritten by Prince, laid out the basic plot for what was then known as *Dreams*: 'This is the story of the dreams and aspirations of 3 individuals' – Morris Day, Vanity and Prince, caught in a love triangle, struggling to find fame on a club circuit that evoked Prince's early days competing with local Minneapolis bands. Emmy-winning screenwriter and TV producer William Blinn was briefly attached to the project, before rookie filmmaker Albert Magnoli – whose 1979 short, *Jazz*, marked the extent of his experience – was called up to the director's chair.

What Prince had been describing as 'an alternative cult movie – we're just going to take our fans with us' had the potential, in Magnoli's eyes, to be a mainstream hit. 'He had this idea that it could be like *Rocky*,' Lisa Coleman says. 'Only a rock'n'roll film ... Something that you invest in and then has a pay-out.' Removing elements like the lead character's schizophrenia and his parents' murder-suicide, Magnoli pitched the outline of what would become *Purple Rain* to an astonished Prince. 'You've only known me for ten minutes, yet you tell me basically my story,' he told the director. 'How is that possible?'

Magnoli was in, but now other key members were out. Frustrated with Jam and Lewis's sacking, Time keyboardist Monte Moir quit the group (Mark Cardenas and Paul Peterson filled in on keyboards, and Jerry Hubbard took on the bass). Morris Day, himself on the verge of walking away, eventually gave in to 'the ultimate show-biz fantasy': 'All my anger at Prince, all my frustrations at his controlling nature melted away once I heard the word *movie*,' he recalled.

Vanity, however, was becoming increasingly unhappy. 'She wanted much more from Prince than he was willing to give her – in a lot of different ways,' Brenda Bennett says. Working with her own agent and Prince's publicist, Howard Bloom, in order to set herself up 'as a separate entity', she gave him an ultimatum: $10 million – more than Prince himself was getting for the movie – or she was out of the picture. 'He called her bluff, or she called his bluff, and she walked.'

Out of 'thousands' of hopefuls, twenty-two-year-old Patricia Kotero got the gig, but her sweeter, more demure personality – 'more of the homey, pretty-girl-next-door quality' – required not only a retooling of the script, but a reworking of the second Vanity 6 album, which had almost been completed. (*Purple Rain* 'was a mega hit when it was released', Brenda says, but if they had filmed that first script, with Prince and Vanity's chemistry on screen, 'it would have been blown out of the water. It would have been a music film, but it would have been a *drama* as well.')

Rechristened Apollonia, after Michael Corleone's first wife in *The Godfather*, Kotero headed Susan Moonsie and Brenda in Apollonia 6, whose debut album left songs like 'Vibrator' and 'G-Spot' in the can in favour of material that better suited the group's new frontwoman.

With much of May through to November 1983 taken up by preparations for filming, Prince, The Time and Apollonia 6 attended daily acting and dance classes. Cramming years' worth of professional training into a handful of months, exercises included pretending to melt like an ice cream or miming being inside an invisible box. 'It could have been a movie in itself,' Lisa Coleman says. 'We were a bunch of goofballs going into a dance class with trench coats on and jumping through the air.'

In the evenings, Prince ran his band through rehearsals that often doubled as recording sessions in a former pet food storage facility in St. Louis Park. Splitting his time between the warehouse, his home studio and LA's Sunset Sound, days started at 10am and often ran until 6am the following morning. 'He was *constantly* on output,' says Susan Rogers, who, newly hired that August, initially as a technician before Prince put her in the engineer's seat, was tasked with setting up recording equipment in the warehouse ('This is something that no one in LA would have done without a team of technicians,' she says). With the 'control room' in the centre of the cement building, Prince again prioritized capturing the essence of his ideas over sonic fidelity.

Songs like 'Let's Go Crazy' were done 'top to bottom' at the warehouse, Rogers recalls, as Prince would bring a basic chord progression or melody and let the others come up with their own parts. 'He *loved* that,' Rogers says. 'He would spend so much time with his band, pulling their ideas. He was a great bandleader.'

When a song was nearing completion, he'd call a break, take a cassette mix to his car and write the lyrics. Other songs came out of jams of hits by artists like James Brown, The Cars or Culture Club which would 'morph into something new'. The ballads – 'The Beautiful Ones', 'Computer Blue' – were recorded in his home studio, 'in his off time, before or after rehearsal'. After working out an idea on the piano, Prince, with the whole arrangement in his head, would tape the lyrics to a mic stand and record the entire drum track with no accompaniment – 'No headphones. He's playing the breaks and the fills. He's playing the whole thing!' Rogers says. Then she'd hand him the bass, or he'd head upstairs to the piano; then he'd add guitar and any other instrumentation before recording his vocals. 'It's so frickin' awesome. He was a young man in the full bloom of his artistry and his success … And it wasn't uncommon for him at four or five o'clock in the morning to put up fresh tape and go around again.'

On the rare occasions that he took a break, Prince would step outside to play basketball – still in his high heels – or challenge people to a game of ping-pong or pool. If he felt like dancing, he would head for Thursday's weekly funk night at First Avenue, a local club where he often tested new material, and which would soon become the focal point of the *Purple Rain* movie, putting Minneapolis on the global stage. 'Sometimes he'd bring a date back with him,' Rogers says, 'but the poor thing would have to sit there while he was working. Nothing mattered more to him than taking advantage of the state his brain was in.'

In addition to his new album, Prince recorded a third Time record – *Ice Cream Castle*, named after a lyric in an early Joni Mitchell song, 'Both Sides, Now' – as well as the Apollonia 6 record. *Ice Cream Castle* included two set-piece songs from the film, 'Jungle Love' and 'The Bird', while *Apollonia 6* featured 'Sex Shooter', the only Vanity 6 song to survive the cull.

Meanwhile, the first the public would hear of the new music Prince had worked up for *Purple Rain* was on 8 August 1983, when he held a benefit concert at First Avenue for the Minneapolis Dance Theater Company, which had provided dance lessons for the cast. The event also saw him unveil his new band: The Revolution. Having been informally referenced on the cover of *1999* (their name written backwards within the '1' that provided the 'I' of his name), the group began to take shape during the *1999* tour, when Prince discovered guitarist Wendy Melvoin, then travelling with Lisa, a childhood friend with whom she'd begun a relationship. 'That she and Lisa were lovers … he's got white, he's got Black, he's got Jewish, he's got non-Jewish, and now he's got a gay faction,' says Brenda Bennett. 'So it's another part of his we're-all-here-together aspect of things.'

Prince invited Wendy to sit in on soundchecks when Dez Dickerson stopped showing. 'All of a sudden, this little girl comes in and she's funky as hell, plus she can play like Joni Mitchell,' Coleman says. Realizing she could be a female Keith Richards to his Mick Jagger, Prince, who had been wondering how to replace Dez, 'was just like, "I've got my answer."'

During the epochal seventy-minute First Avenue show, Prince debuted five *Purple Rain* songs: 'Let's Go Crazy', 'Computer Blue', 'I Would Die 4 U', 'Baby I'm a Star' and 'Purple Rain' itself. 'It was super intense and dark and sweaty,' Coleman recalls. 'There was something special in the energy.'

Prince's own confidence in the performance – and his new line-up – became clear when that night's live recordings of 'I Would Die 4 U', 'Baby I'm a Star' and 'Purple Rain' were used as the final three tracks on the *Purple Rain* album.

The movie began shooting in November 1983 and lasted throughout the notoriously cold Minneapolis winter, during which cast members, waking at four in the morning to start their cars, could discover two feet of snow on the ground and three inches of ice on their windows. ('With the wind chill, it was like seventy below zero,' Coleman says.)

Boosted by an extra round of funding from a newly convinced Warner Bros Pictures, filming ended in December, with some re-shooting in Los Angeles. What hit the screens on 27 July 1984 was light years away from the handwritten treatment Prince had initially drafted. Although the basic psychological exploration of Prince's character – now renamed The Kid – remained intact, his romantic struggles, parental issues, creative tensions – both within his own band and with his rivals – and rise to fame fed into a narrative arc that cannily reframed Prince as the star he had worked to become, while also offering a portrait that was more autobiographical than he would admit. (When asked about his portrayal as an abusive husband, John L. demurred: he 'never used a gun'.)

Although the film spilled into melodrama, it also revealed Morris Day to be an excellent comic actor – even if some of that comedy attracted criticism for its misogyny, particularly a scene in which Jerome Benton throws a girlfriend of Day's into a dumpster. 'Sometimes, for the sake of humour, we may have gone overboard,' Prince told MTV. 'Those gestures were in line with what the young men at that time thought was funny and "fair play",' Susan Rogers says. 'We have to give him credit for being the product of his time ... For having the narrow vision that we all have when we're young.'

Purple Rain's live performances, with flashy cuts and outlandish fashions that heightened their immediacy, sold the film to a mainstream audience seeking the thrill of MTV pop promos on the big screen. After an opening weekend that pulled in $7.3 million – easily recouping the cost of production en route to a $70 million gross – *Purple Rain*'s distribution went from two hundred to nine hundred cinemas across the US. Preceded by the single release of 'When Doves Cry', on 16 May in the US (a month later in the UK), and the *Purple Rain* soundtrack album on 25 June (also following a month later in the UK), the film's success made Prince the first artist since The Beatles to simultaneously hold a No. 1 movie, single and album release in the States, with the album selling thirteen million copies in the US alone and knocking Bruce Springsteen's *Born in the USA* off the top spot. It remained there for twenty-four weeks.

The frenzy surrounding the album's release disguised one thing: *Purple Rain* was one of the strangest records to not only become a major hit, but to impact pop culture on such a global scale. Back-masked messages promising the return of the Lord; dispassionately delivered, seemingly coded questions regarding water temperature; psycho-sexual dramas that, in their honesty and intensity, had never been attempted in pop music before: Prince wove these into a cohesive whole. And while he may have rocked harder, or been infectiously funkier elsewhere, *Purple Rain* is where he entwined the two to perfection.

'I think *Purple Rain* is the most avant-garde purple thing I've ever done,' Prince reflected to *Ebony* magazine in 1986. Singling out 'When Doves Cry' and 'Let's Go Crazy', he noted: 'Most Black artists wouldn't try a groove like that,' adding, 'I'm not saying that I'm great or anything like that; I'm just saying that I'm an alternative. I'm something else.'

'When Doves Cry' *was* something else. Unusually, Prince had spent two days on the song, building a 'huge, mega thing' out of synthesizers and raging guitars. 'And pretty soon he started un-producing it,' Peggy McCreary says. 'He started taking instruments out, and at the very end he punched the bass out. And I looked at him and he said, "Nobody's gonna believe I've got the nerve to do this."' The result was a strangely weightless, otherworldly feeling at the centre of ping-ponging synths and an echoing drum machine, over which Prince sang lyrics that laid out the movie's narrative themes.

Marylou Badeaux recalls the label's reaction: 'What the eff do we do with this? Radio will never accept this.'

It became the first single since Michael Jackson's 'Billie Jean' to top the Hot 100, Black and Dance/Disco charts.

'Suddenly, pop radio said, "He's ours,"' says Badeaux. 'And they were a big part of helping how big the movie was.'

* * * * *

With the *Purple Rain* album being formally credited to Prince & The Revolution, the group – Wendy and Lisa, Bobby Z., BrownMark and Dr. Fink – were elevated to a level of fame that paralleled Prince's. And with the film highlighting their electrifying stage show, fans flocked to see it for themselves. 'We wanted to make them feel like they were in the movie,' Roy Bennett says. 'To be able to have multiple theatrical vignettes … recreating the emotion of the live performances.'

Creating an immersive experience – lights and sound coming from all sides of the arena venues Prince was now filling; dropping flowers on the audience at the start of each concert – Bennett helped Prince realize his most ambitious stage show yet for a ninety-eight-date trek that opened in Detroit, traversed the US and saw him sell out a week's worth of nights in many cities. 'We were just on another planet,' Bennett recalls. 'When you have an arena full of women screaming, there's no sound in the world like that anywhere.'

During one flight, with the band acclimatizing to Learjets and limos after years of travelling in station wagons and carrying their own bags, Prince, sitting with a stack of 'a hundred magazines' and 'doing everything he could to really experience what was happening', told Lisa: 'I'm not going to miss a single thing.'

Heightening the atmosphere, the audiences came dressed as though they were extras at First Avenue, while Prince took to the stage in all his purple majesty – Little Richard pompadour, Jimi Hendrix ruffles – every inch the modern dandy, his very existence a conflation of his life and art. 'He really understood what it took to be a rock star,' Bennett says. 'His persona was that level onstage. His persona was that level offstage, too.' Not everyone was along for the ride. Morris Day, wanting to 'be my own man, not Prince's puppet', as he later recalled, quit after *Purple Rain* wrapped. Splitting for LA, he had 'no notion of rebuilding The Time. Or any other band,' but instead pursued a solo career.

Although Apollonia 6 could be spotted on stage with The Revolution some nights, they had effectively broken up. After the first edit of a filmed mini-musical, *Happy Birthday, Mr. Christian*, failed to convince Prince ('He hated it – he just threw it on the shelf and then walked away,' Brenda Bennett says), Apollonia decided to pursue acting over singing, while Susan Moonsie left the limelight altogether.

A Brenda Bennett-fronted iteration of the group, Pandora 6 – with Jill Jones and Wendy Melvoin's twin sister, Susannah, in a supporting role – was briefly considered, but became swallowed up by the sheer number of projects Prince was juggling. 'Everybody was crashing,' Bennett recalls. 'He said, "It's not gonna happen right now; I've got things going on. But hang in there."'

The *Purple Rain* tour's support slot went instead to percussionist Sheila E., daughter of Latin jazz musician Pete Escovedo. Newly involved, romantically as well as musically (she had provided backing vocals to the 'Let's Go

Crazy' B-side 'Erotic City'), Prince found the time to record Sheila's debut album, *The Glamorous Life*, in the wake of the shooting of *Purple Rain*. 'She was such a talented musician, so he had a rapport with her that he didn't have with a lot of others because she was doing it from the time she was walking,' Peggy McCreary says. 'I would watch them bounce off each other – it was a fun energy.'

After years of pushing the boundaries of permissibility, Prince's growing fame made him a target for those with more conservative values. While listening to *Purple Rain* with her eleven-year-old daughter, Tipper Gore, the wife of US Democratic senator (and future Vice President) Al Gore, was outraged at the reference to masturbation in 'Darling Nikki''s opening verse. Along with three other women, whose husbands were connected with the Republican Party, she formed the Parents Music Resource Center, a committee that lobbied the Recording Industry Association of America to adopt a classification system for music. As part of their campaign, they compiled the 'Filthy Fifteen': a roll-call of songs containing potentially offensive content. Topping the list: 'Darling Nikki'; below it: 'Sugar Walls', another Prince song, penned for Scottish pop singer Sheena Easton (it wasn't about the house in *Hansel and Gretel*). The PMRC's efforts would eventually result in the introduction of 'Parental Advisory: Explicit Content' stickers on releases deemed unsuitable for young audiences.

Having declared himself 'your messiah' in 'I Would Die 4 U', Prince was conscious of assuming a new role for the biggest audiences of his career to date. If the *Purple Rain* album was arguably more sensual than sexual, Prince's live shows revealed a divide between his reputation for deviancy and a new impulse towards promoting moral decency; before hitting the stage, he held communal prayer sessions. 'Being somebody that was always controversial and making people think, and having that edge slightly disappeared,' Roy Bennett says. Over a decade later, in the 1990s, and on the verge of a radical religious conversion, Prince revealed that an earlier version of 'Let's Go Crazy' 'was about God and the de-elevation of sin. But the problem was that religion as a subject is taboo in pop music.' He added: 'People think that the records they release have got to be hip, but what I need to do is tell the truth.'

In the studio, a pattern developed as Prince dealt with a growing conflict between his sexuality and his spirituality: 'When he would be *really* salacious,' Susan Rogers notes, 'he would follow that with either an admission of guilt or some sort of contrition.' Apologizing for his lust, he would 'weave into his music expressions of gratitude to God'. This manifested itself on stage during the *Purple Rain* tour as a nightly confrontation between Prince and his maker, with Prince caught in a spotlight and God's voice represented by thunderous piano. 'I know I said I'd be good,' Prince would plead. 'But they dig it when I'm bad.'

It was a mini-drama that he would explore on his next album, hints of which came towards the end of the *Purple Rain* tour – not that anyone beyond his closest confidants knew it. Although both band and management tried to convince him to take the show overseas, Prince, exhausted from five months on the road, pulled the plug on the *Purple Rain* experience. 'Holy *hell* was he ever eager to get off that tour,' Susan Rogers says of the final shows. 'He's rushing through things … the way he's talking to the audience, he just wants *outta there*.'

On 2 April 1985, just five days before completing the tour, Steve Fargnoli announced Prince's decision to retire from live performance 'for an indeterminate number of years'. Asked what he planned to do instead, Prince offered: 'I'm going to look for the ladder.'

5

Paisley Overground

There wasn't much warning: Warner Bros's biggest star was on his way. When Prince arrived at the LA office, he was dressed in a purple kimono and carried a rose. Surrounded by bodyguards and management, with Wendy and Lisa scattering petals as they went, he led everyone to a conference room hastily decked out in purple balloons and white streamers. A large table had been removed in order to accommodate label execs and other guests, including Joni Mitchell and Prince's father, for the premiere of his new album. The sound of finger cymbals, darbuka, cello and an oud filled the air; the songs had a pronounced psychedelic feel. There were no arena-friendly singalongs.

With Prince sitting on the floor, the execs around him started to shift their feet. 'The body language of it was very clear,' Marylou Badeaux recalls. 'You could sense a tenseness.' Prince just looked down. 'He had a very, very strong sixth sense … And he knew.' After the last note, he got up and left. No words, no explanation.

A pop promoter approached Badeaux that afternoon, anxious about getting the new music on to radio. 'He doesn't see that as his problem. He sees that as your problem,' Badeaux told the promoter. 'You didn't think you were gonna get *Purple Rain 2*, did you?'

'He knew that *Purple Rain* was something that would always be there for him,' Lisa Coleman says, 'but it wasn't the gold watch at the end of a career. It was a new beginning … he just had to keep his head down and keep working if he was gonna be the great Prince that he wanted to be.'

This was late February 1985. Bored with *Purple Rain*, but with another month and a half of touring ahead of him, Prince wanted to get his new work out there as soon as possible. He'd already been sitting on it since December, after finishing final overdubs and mixes with Susan Rogers in a mobile recording truck parked outside his house as Christmas Eve rolled into the early hours of Christmas Day.

In January, he'd won Favorite Album in the American Music Awards' Soul/R&B Album and Pop/Rock Album categories, while 'When Doves Cry' had scored Favorite Soul/R&B Single, with the *Purple Rain* album on its way to earning two Grammys and an Oscar.

But while all expectations were on maximizing the album's potential, for Prince, expectations were irrelevant – which is how he came to skip the recording of 'We Are the World', scheduled to take place right after the AMAs in the early hours of 29 January. Organized by the legendary producer Quincy Jones, the charity recording was set to raise money in aid of famine relief in Ethiopia. Under the collective name USA for Africa, a diverse array of artists entered the A&M studio that night, passing a sign that instructed them to 'Check your egos at the door'; Bob Dylan, Bruce Springsteen, Stevie Wonder, Diana Ross, Lionel Richie and Michael Jackson, Prince's rival for the 1980s pop crown, were among them. As they sang in unity, however, with a space held for him next to Jackson, Prince was having dinner with protégé and on-off girlfriend Jill Jones at a Mexican restaurant, Carlos'n Charlie's, on Sunset Boulevard. Sheila E. was sent to the studio in his place.

When, at the end of the night, a paparazzo tried to get into Prince's limo, looking for a scoop on rock royalty's charity no-show, bodyguards ejected him. 'Dude bumps his head, drops his camera,' Susan Rogers recalls. One of the bodyguards, Wally Safford, 'throws a couple hundred bucks at him, pays him off and off they go'.

Addressing his absence, Prince later explained, 'I probably would have just clammed up with so many great people in the room.' Rather than ducking out on the night, however, he'd declined Quincy's invitation in advance, first offering to contribute guitar to the song ('They told him, "No, we've got Greg Phillinganes,"' Rogers laughs) and then agreeing to donate a new song, '4 the Tears in Your Eyes', to the *We Are the World* album.

'I think it was cool he didn't do "We Are the World",' Bob Merlis says. 'He's not a joiner ... You got all these other stars, don't worry about it.' But the damage was done: seemingly cut off from the world and hiding behind his bodyguards, the biggest star on the planet appeared to be suffering from an outsized ego.

It didn't help that his head of security, Big Chick, had been involved in a previous incident: an altercation outside a Sheila E. concert that past September had left a photographer seeking $2.75 million in damages. Quitting Prince's employ following the latest fracas, Chick needed some quick cash to help fund a cocaine addiction sizeable even for a man of his build and sold a tell-all interview to the *National Enquirer*. Under the headline 'The Real Prince: He's Trapped in a Bizarre Secret World of Terror', Chick claimed, among other things, that Prince lived in an armed fortress, barricaded from reality.

Although not barricaded, Prince had withdrawn, even from those closest to him. 'He took it in really deeply,' Lisa Coleman says of his fame. 'And in a difficult way it separated him from us more. That was hard on us – and I'm sure it was a little bit hard on him, too.' While travelling in separate buses had been 'kind of fun, like the teacher wasn't in class', The Revolution also began to question their roles; the days of going to the movies together or roller-skating around Minneapolis's lakes were over. 'Are we just hired hands, or are we a band?' Coleman wondered.

Meanwhile, the young talent who used to borrow his manager's car to get around, and once entered Sunset Sound giggling because he'd been recognized by a fan, now had his BMW and *Purple Rain* motorbike trucked in, or would turn up in a purple limo. But constructing what Susan Rogers saw as a 'psychic wall' was crucial to conserving himself for his art. 'That allowed him to walk, basically psychically unmolested, into the public arena ... He realized at some point: I don't have to answer the questions. Let them figure it out. And he was brave enough to let them get it wrong ... He never defended himself.' It also 'added to the mystique', Marylou Badeaux says. 'People couldn't get enough of him.' They 'were like, "Well, he's just saving himself for me."'

Creatively, however, Prince was at his most open, and began courting Wendy and Lisa's musical input with more frequency. While rounding out ideas in the studio, the duo became confidants as Prince developed an increasingly serious relationship with Wendy's sister, Susannah. During sessions for his *Purple Rain* follow-up, she introduced him to The Beatles and Led Zeppelin. Wendy, meanwhile, turned him on to her favourite Brazilian music. Lisa's knowledge of classical music expanded his world in another direction.

'We were very close and spent a lot of time together and nourished each other a lot,' Coleman says. 'He trusted me and Wendy to work in the studio either with him or even when he wasn't there.' While Prince 'had the melody and the lyrics and the groove' himself, Wendy and Lisa provided 'the stuff in between' – the colour and instrumental nuances that characterized his new work.

When the *Around the World in a Day* album was released, on 22 April 1985, just weeks after the *Purple Rain* tour closed, it revealed the first flowerings of this artistic expansion. It was Lisa's harpsichord part that formed the basis for 'Raspberry Beret', while her brother, David Coleman, had written the album's title track and was responsible for the Middle Eastern instrumentation that startled Warner Bros.

Elsewhere, utopian visions ('Paisley Park') sat alongside critiques of fame ('Pop Life'), exquisite ballads ('Condition of the Heart'), a celebration of the loss of virginity ('Raspberry Beret') and a paean to masturbation ('Tamborine' – couched in far more playful language than the censors-baiting 'Darling Nikki'), while the album's penultimate track, 'The Ladder', addressed a king's search for salvation in a land of sin, going some way towards unpacking Prince's cryptic retirement statement. The album's closing song, 'Temptation', underlined his mindset: after a raunchy seven minutes, the ominous coda found him – newly in love with Susannah Melvoin, though still unable to resist his libidinous urges – re-enacting his nightly conversations with God, with the deity sentencing him to death for pursuing sex rather than love.

Recalling the heyday of 1960s psychedelic rock while weaving his disparate influences into an out-and-out pop album – 'He was a genius with melody and a genius with rhythm,' Susan Rogers says, 'but in his heart of hearts he was a *pop* musician. He played hooks' – *Around the World in a Day* was hailed as a bold creative leap, particularly given its astonishingly speedy turnaround. 'It's true that I record very fast,' Prince told MTV. Adding praise for Wendy and Lisa – 'It goes even quicker now that the girls help me' – he also refuted Big Chick's revelations: 'I don't live in a prison. I am not afraid of anything.'

New musical experiences weren't the only influence, either: a one-time experiment with hallucinogens informed the album. It wasn't 'a massive thing', says Roy Bennett. Prince had become 'fascinated' by the pioneering musicians of the 1960s and 'loved what that world was and … just wanted to explore it'. *Around the World in a Day* 'was meant to be more like a world album – like an international thing', Coleman says. 'It wasn't, "Go into your head and do drugs." It was more like: "Get out in the world and meet people."'

Around the World in a Day hit No. 1 on *Billboard*'s Top Pop Albums chart, but failed to replicate its predecessor's chart-topping performance on the Top Black Albums chart, where it stalled at No. 4. Selling fewer copies than *Purple Rain*, its sales were hampered by Prince's initial refusal to release a single, film a promo video or even allow Warner Bros to advertise its existence. In need of a boost, however, he finally relented. But for anyone disappointed that Prince had delivered the anti-*Purple Rain* record, he had a clear response: 'I don't *want* to make an album like the earlier ones. Wouldn't it be cool to put your albums back-to-back and not get bored?'

* * * * *

Staving off that boredom, Prince kept on making music. 'You couldn't always tell when one record stopped and the next one started,' Susan Rogers says. Once he hit upon the songs that provided 'the seed' for a project, it became easier to decide what tracks would fit around them to form an album. Meanwhile, with Michael Jackson 'right outside his door' and Run-DMC 'breathing down his neck' with a hard-edged sound that paved the way for hip-hop's ascent into the mainstream, confidence and 'sheer willpower' kept Prince awake.

'I've come to believe that Prince was biologically built to be creative,' says Rogers, who would tease him for being a lightweight who could 'get high on a Coca-Cola'. Whereas most other artists would have to rely on amphetamines and other stimulants to sustain his pace, Prince 'was not taking drugs for recreational purpose'. His competitive spirit drove those around him to keep going, too:

'If he's staying up, there's *no way* he's gonna be able to say that I can't hang with him,' Rogers says.

A second Sheila E. album, *Romance 1600*, had been completed by early 1985, along with the self-titled album by his latest side project, The Family. Salvaged from the ashes of The Time, The Family found a hesitant 'St.' Paul Peterson promoted from keyboardist to frontman duties alongside Susannah Melvoin. Having opened Prince up to new influences in art, Susannah would soon take him down an entirely unforeseen path: when the couple became engaged in the summer of 1985, it seemed as though she had convinced the promiscuous star to settle down.

Still musically restless, however, Prince searched for more territory to conquer. Having asked Alan Leeds's brother, saxophonist Eric Leeds, to join The Revolution for the *Purple Rain* tour, Prince now sought his expertise in jazz music, with Eric introducing him to landmark Miles Davis and John Coltrane albums of the 1960s. Released two weeks apart in August 1985, the Sheila E. and The Family albums revealed tentative steps towards absorbing new avant-garde styles into Prince's own music. Sheila's saxophonist, Eddie M., ran rampant on her album, while Eric Leeds was an official member of The Family, whose breezy pop-funk was set against curious arrangements that marked yet another new addition to Prince's sonic palette: orchestral parts written by Clare Fischer, a composer who had previously worked with long-time Prince favourites Rufus (whose frontwoman, Chaka Khan, had enjoyed a 1984 solo hit with a cover of the *Prince* album's 'I Feel for You').

Although he'd included small ensembles of cello, violin and viola on *Purple Rain* and *Around the World in a Day*, Prince was thrilled with his new collaborator's large-scale orchestrations and established a superstitious working method that lasted until Fischer's death in January 2012: sharing their work from a distance, for fear that meeting in person would weaken their creative bond. The result of their first collaboration, The Family's album also included one of Prince's most enduring songs, 'Nothing Compares 2 U', a haunting ballad taken at a funereal pace underscored by ethereal synth lines. Tucked away on a side-project record, the song became a global hit when Irish singer Sinéad O'Connor released a version of it in 1990.

With the Jazz Age on his mind, Prince set about planning his second feature film. Shot on the French Riviera from September through to November 1985, *Under the Cherry Moon* swapped musical numbers for farcical set pieces in a black-and-white romantic comedy set in a fantasy 1920s. Taking the lead role, Prince played Christopher Tracy, a gigolo who decides to swindle, then falls in love with, a young heiress, Mary Sharon, only to be killed, by order of her father. 'There was a big fight about that one,' Marylou Badeaux recalls. Warner Bros didn't want Prince's character to die, but Prince was 'dead set on doing it, and wouldn't take no for an answer'. Realizing 'they didn't have a decent movie anyway', the label gave up: 'Let him die!'

For Prince, the matter seemed to go beyond mere story-telling. Increasingly devoted to Susannah Melvoin, it was as if he sought to lay his raffish past to rest. But Susannah lost out on the role of Mary Sharon, which was given to Kristin

Scott Thomas, a perky newcomer who accepted it as her breakout lead part. Before long, with Prince starting affairs with both Scott Thomas and French co-star Emmanuelle Sallet, Susannah was sent back home. 'He wasn't ready for commitment with just one person at that time,' Susan Rogers says. 'Their engagement was on and off.'

Rounding out the principal cast was Jerome Benton. Free from his duties as a dancer with The Family, who had played just one concert that August (after which Paul Peterson left, frustrated with feeling that Prince's priorities lay elsewhere), Benton played Christopher's comic foil, Tricky.

Having brushed off a number of proposed scripts, and with his first choice of director, French fashion photographer and music-video director Jean-Baptiste Mondino, unavailable, Prince hired the inexperienced Becky Johnston to write a screenplay, picking Mary Lambert – whose biggest credits to date included two Madonna promo videos, plus the video for Sheila E.'s 'The Glamorous Life' – to direct. When Lambert was demoted to 'creative consultant' ('It makes no sense for me to stand between him and the film,' she said), Prince installed himself as director, figuring, 'A movie is … just a larger version of an album.'

'Just because he made great records doesn't mean he knew how to make a movie,' Bob Merlis says. 'It didn't flow. You couldn't just get into the action.' *Under the Cherry Moon*'s premiere set the tone for the film's reception. Opening on 1 July 1986 in Sheridan, Wyoming, the hometown of Lisa Barber, a local hotel maid and the lucky 10,000th caller to an MTV competition, the event was: 'rock'n'roll superstar comes to your goofball town and everybody's involved',

Merlis recalls. It took three flights to get there from LA: 'All these groovy executive types who work for MTV get off the plane, and it's just cowboys everywhere and nothing makes sense … This guy's gonna end up being pulled in the back of a pickup truck if he doesn't keep his mouth shut.'

The movie's inaugural viewing was followed by a concert at Sheridan's Holiday Inn. One local's observation – 'We don't care about no boy who wears tight pants and struts around like a woman' – presaged the wider public's reaction to the film. Although *Under the Cherry Moon* finds Prince at arguably his most playful and relaxed on screen, drawing praise from *The Village Voice* for his ability to 'hold a film simply with the force of his personality', it nevertheless won five Golden Raspberry awards (out of eight nominations) and was, as the *San Jose Mercury News* put it, an 'unmitigated display of narcissism'. For Prince, however, it merely affirmed his own creative vision: 'I learned that I can't direct what I didn't write.'

By contrast, *Under the Cherry Moon*'s soundtrack album, *Parade*, was greeted with superlatives. Released three months before the film, Prince had recorded the album's first four songs in one sitting, telling Peggy McCreary and Susan Rogers to just keep the tape rolling until he said stop. Channelling his recent explorations in jazz, *Parade*'s stripped-down funk verged on the abstract. This resulted in an artistic high-water mark that was, ironically, kept off the US top spot by *Control*, the first Janet Jackson album produced by Jimmy Jam and Terry Lewis, the former Time members whose own hitmaking take on the 'Minneapolis sound' would soon make them household names.

Prince almost passed on *Parade*'s biggest hit, 'Kiss' – Warner Bros, too, when they heard it. Like 'When Doves Cry', it didn't have a bassline, and the label thought it sounded like a demo. Actually originally demoed as an acoustic blues number, Prince had given 'Kiss' to Mazarati, an R&B band who, mentored by BrownMark and David Rivkin, were recording in the studio next door to him at Sunset Sound. After hearing their radical new arrangement – juddering synths, propulsive beat – Prince reclaimed the song, paring it back to a sparse future-funk that became a transatlantic No. 1 and also took him to the top of the Hot 100 and the Hot Black Singles charts for the first time in two years.

Mazarati had to make do with '100 MPH', which just made it into the Top 20 on the Black chart. Meanwhile, requests for hits kept coming: The Bangles had picked up on 'Manic Monday', once pegged for Apollonia 6 (it settled at No. 2, just beneath 'Kiss'). Former bandmate André Cymone received 'The Dance Electric', a Top 10 Hot Black Singles chart entry. Country star Kenny Rogers recorded 'You're My Love', a song that dated back to 1982.

Having begun work on Jill Jones's self-titled debut album that same year, Prince continued to shape the record through to the end of 1986. Finally emerging in May 1987, it fell under the radar of all but the most committed Prince fans. Those who did hear the record, however, felt it was worth the wait: songs such as 'All Day, All Night' and 'Baby, You're a Trip' made it a highlight among his side-project work, and the last in a run of essential protégé albums.

Searching for his own next full-length project, Prince had recorded – and shelved – a pair of instrumental jazz-funk sessions with various band members under the name The Flesh, before turning his attention to *Dream Factory*, the planned follow-up to *Parade*, which was fast expanding into a carnivalesque double album that would mark the peak of The Revolution's creative input. He'd even convinced Warner Bros to finance his own record label, Paisley Park Records. But Prince was more interested in making music than he was in building a roster and running a label. 'You can be Berry Gordy, but you can't be Berry Gordy *and* Marvin Gaye at the same time,' Bob Merlis says. Warner Bros viewed the enterprise as a vanity label for girlfriend projects that neither side were committed to promoting. 'Paisley Park was sort of like, "I'll put all my" – excuse me – "bitches here,"' Marylou Badeaux says.

With *Under the Cherry Moon* tanking (Warner had recouped less than a third of their $10 million investment) and *Parade* soaring, Prince was coaxed out of the studio in order to take the album on tour. Distracted by his new music, however, and reluctant to commit to a punishing *Purple Rain*-style itinerary, he staged a ten-date jaunt throughout March and April in the US – maximizing hype and sales by announcing venues a matter of hours before showtime. Having fallen in love with Europe – 'the elegance about it, the sophistication about it … was a stimulation for him', says Roy Bennett – while filming *Under the Cherry Moon*, and preferring the way that continental audiences reacted to his music, he took The Revolution to the UK, Europe and Japan for his first overseas arena concerts.

A money-saving back-to-basics show that had more in common with soul revues than the high-concept performances of his recent tours, Prince's new set-up also lent itself to a pair of secret aftershow gigs held in smaller London venues during the early hours of the morning. Freed from the expectations of large audiences, he ran The Revolution through looser, more improvised sets before his most devoted fans; in years to come, you-had-to-be-there stories would make the aftershows hotter tickets than the main events themselves.

Their time on the road may have been limited, but The Revolution had expanded. Dubbed the 'Bugs Bunny Revue' by the original members, the group's live line-up now included dancers turned bodyguards Wally Safford and Greg Brooks; Sheila E. and her guitarist Miko Weaver; new recruit Matt 'Atlanta Bliss' Blistan on trumpet, alongside saxophonist Eric Leeds; and Susannah Melvoin and Jerome Benton on backing vocals. But 'congas and dancers and back-up singers and horns' didn't feel part of 'the cause', Lisa Coleman says. 'We were like, "We don't need this shit."' Feeling underappreciated and underpaid, the group were asked to sign 'bare minimum' contracts. 'We were expendable as far as they were concerned,' Coleman says. 'It was really kind of insulting, especially to Wendy and I, who were doing so much work,' not just in the studio, but also as musical directors, teaching new songs to the band.

Meanwhile, Prince's fracturing relationship with Susannah created extra tension with Wendy and Lisa. 'Prince got really quiet – especially with me,' Coleman says. While he would have intense discussions with Wendy about her sister, Coleman felt 'like an innocent bystander' being forced to pick a side: him, or the Melvoins. 'I felt that he was angry with me, and that made me angry with him,' she says. 'We really all kind of knew that this was a bad situation, and I don't know if we can pull out of it.'

After the final *Parade* show, at Japan's Yokohama Stadium, on 9 September, Prince smashed his white 'cloud guitar' and left the stage. 'That was his *Purple Rain* guitar – it represented Prince & The Revolution and *Purple Rain*,' Coleman says. 'And to see him smash not only one, but two? He's more than rocking hard right now. He's trying to say something.'

The following month, he invited Wendy and Lisa to the house he was renting in Beverly Hills for the winter; after dinner, he made a call to Bobby Z.: Sheila E. was taking his place. Inviting Wendy and Lisa up to his bedroom, he finally came out and said it: they were being sacked, too.

'He said he needed to go back and do things by himself more,' Coleman says. In the two years since *Purple Rain*, his closest collaborators had become too big; he could no longer ask them to wear what he wanted and perform how he expected. 'Our roles weren't going to change. They had grown and solidified into a certain thing. And for him to move forward, he just felt like: "I can't ask you guys to change,"' Coleman says. 'It was like breaking up with my boyfriend. I felt really sad and heartbroken.' A dissatisfied BrownMark quit, leaving Matt Fink as the sole original member of the group. The Revolution was over – and, with it, a collaborative period that had taken Prince on an unprecedented artistic run.

'The decision to disband The Revolution was a pruning of his creative tree,' Susan Rogers says. 'It apparently made more sense to him to have the tree grow in new directions and … to focus on the strength of the trunk, rather than the strength of the branches. So he returned to the thing that was never going to leave him: himself and his own creativity.'

* * * * *

Revisiting the *Dream Factory* recordings, Prince stripped them of The Revolution's parts. 'That's what we had been working on pretty consistently,' Coleman says. 'I guess it just freaked Prince out a little bit.'

Re-recording parts himself and laying down new songs in the studio installed in his new home, a three-storey, mansion-style property situated on thirty acres of land at 7141 Galpin Boulevard in Chanhassen, the project took on a radically different shape that sought to mask even Prince's own involvement. Collecting eight tracks sung in a style Prince had discovered in 1984 while recording 'Erotic City' – by slowing down the tape when he recorded his vocals, his voice would sound eerily high-pitched when played back at the normal speed – Prince prepared the songs for release in the new year, simply under the name Camille, an alter ego of indeterminate gender, likely named after the nineteenth-century French intersex figure Herculine Barbin, who had also gone by the pseudonym.

But with ideas for new projects arriving daily, Prince began to entirely rethink what his next work should be. A planned musical, *The Dawn*, would have pitted two rival bands against each other, while a mooted *Camille* movie would have seen Prince as a schizophrenic character at war with himself. By the end of November 1986, a glut of fresh songs was added to material from the *Dream Factory* and *Camille* projects in order to create a twenty-two-track triple album, *Crystal Ball*.

Like the album itself, the song 'Crystal Ball', a ten-minute, multi-sectioned centrepiece, was the most ambitious thing Prince had ever attempted on record. It was too ambitious for Warner Bros, who refused to take on a costly three-disc set from an artist whose work rate was starting to become an issue. 'People wouldn't buy it 'cause it's too expensive,' Marylou Badeaux says. 'And the next week, he'd have another album – God help us!'

Asking Prince to write an extra song for *1999*, however, had inadvertently resulted in a masterpiece; requesting that he cut tracks from his latest collection did much the same. Removing seven songs and adding one new recording, 'U Got the Look', a duet with Sheena Easton, Prince went back to the label in January 1987 with the double album *Sign o' the Times*. Released two months later, on 30 March, and credited solely to Prince, it was hailed as yet another artistic peak from a man who had already scaled several of them. For Wendy and Lisa, however, whose input had been integral to many of the songs' earlier incarnations, listening to it for the first time was 'horrible. It was like being cut out of the family photo album … That's cold-blooded!'

Sign o' the Times found Prince gleefully cycling through musical styles while testing the limits of his instruments and studio. Despite the album's eighty-minute running time, the individual songs are exercises in restraint: minimalist in their arrangements, with each instrumental element stretched beyond the basic demands of composition, adding textural layers whose sum is greater than their parts.

'Prince isn't just rearranging ordinary songs,' *The New York Times* marvelled. 'He's started to warp the songs themselves.' With an otherworldly and at times murky sound defined by Prince's mastery of the Fairlight CMI synthesizer alongside his Linn LM-1 drum machine, *Sign o' the Times* revealed a maturing worldview – one that explicitly tackled AIDS and poverty (the title track), promised salvation ('The Cross') and rejoiced in monogamy ('Forever in My Life'; the quintessential slow jam 'Adore', whose overlapping, gospel-infused vocal lines offered a master class in soul). If 'It' and 'Hot Thing' made room for Prince's lascivious urges, 'Strange Relationship' laid bare the manipulations and co-dependencies that can make relationships toxic, while 'If I Was Your Girlfriend' offered a far more nuanced exploration of gender roles and trust in a way that few male songwriters had managed before – or have dared since.

While that song 'stopped radio in its tracks', according to Alan Leeds ('Homophobes misinterpreted the lyrics'), 'U Got the Look' and 'I Could Never Take the Place of Your Man' offered exemplary radio-friendly pop-rock. The floor-shaking funk of 'Housequake' should have led the way as a smash hit, but the fact that it was overlooked for single release underscored both the confidence Prince had in the album's other options and his reluctance to take the obvious route into the charts. Peaking at No. 6 in the Top Pop and No. 4 in the Top Black albums charts in the US, *Sign o' the Times* didn't quite match *Parade*'s sales performance, but was hailed as Prince's most dazzling achievement. Proof that he didn't need The Revolution to continue his evolution, the album was, in *Rolling Stone*'s words, an example of 'virtuoso solo eclecticism' that had 'seldom been so abundantly displayed'.

Prince, however, would never forgive Warner Bros for challenging his decision-making in the lead-up to the album: 'Because people at Warners were tired, they came up with reasons why I should be tired, too,' he complained a decade later, referring to their disagreement over *Crystal Ball*. 'I don't know if it's their place to talk me in or out of things.'

Shot in front of a backdrop loaned from a local production of *Guys and Dolls*, the *Sign o' the Times* album cover carried an indication of what should have been: a purple plasma ball glowing on the drum riser. The object assumed the same position on stage, as part of a new set design by Roy Bennett that reflected the album's artwork: neon signs, buildings that lit up as if they had an internal life. It was 'full-on theatre', Roy Bennett says. 'Broadway, but done in a rock'n'roll style.'

Having worked up a loose storyline to play out each night, Prince took his new band – Sheila E., Miko Weaver, Dr. Fink, Eric Leeds and Atlanta Bliss, bolstered by bassist Levi Seacer, Jr., and keyboardist Boni Boyer, with new dancing foil Cat Glover leading Greg and Wally through choreography – on a European tour. With the majority of the group filling their own support slot as Madhouse, an instrumental jazz-funk outfit whose debut album, *8*, had been released in January (a second, *16*, would follow in November), Prince was keen to show off their prowess. Arguably the greatest live outfit he put together, they were more than capable of handling the new songs' myriad demands across a run of thirty-four summer shows that soon ranked among Prince's most exciting.

When he returned to the US, however, Prince settled into Paisley Park, the newly completed development based in Chanhassen, on the outskirts of Minneapolis. Paid for in cash and constructed over an eighteen-month period, it consisted of three recording studios, a soundstage, video-editing equipment, an array of offices and rehearsal rooms, a salon, kitchen and private living quarters away from his main residence on Galpin Boulevard. The 65,000-square-foot complex would become Prince's main base of operations for the rest of his life. 'More than anywhere he's ever lived, it represented so much to him,' Susan Rogers says. 'His life took place within those walls once it was built.'

Editing footage filmed in France, the Netherlands and Belgium for a planned concert movie, Prince felt it didn't capture the nuances needed to bring his storyline to life, and decided to reshoot the majority of the performances on Paisley Park's soundstage. Concert films were known to struggle during the Christmas season, however, so Warner Bros passed on the project, leaving Prince to find another distributor for a nationwide theatrical run that gained unanimous praise but which, commercially, failed to reap the financial benefits of an actual tour.

Refusing to take *Sign o' the Times* around the States was 'one of the biggest mistakes we ever made', Roy Bennett says. Warner Bros, too, felt they needed more time to fully promote 'a two-record set that had the depth of brilliance that record had'. But night after night of singing songs written while he was still in love and living with Susannah Melvoin had taken their toll. His refusal to continue touring 'may have had something to do with depression', says Susan Rogers, whose time with Prince was also coming to an end. 'I think he was struggling. Losing The Revolution and Susannah caused an earthquake that had aftershocks. And I think he just wanted to be done with it – be done with the songs and the look' – peach, a large part of the aesthetic, was Susannah's colour – 'and the attitude that reminded him of them.'

As 1987 came to a close, Prince rang the new year in with a $200-a-ticket benefit concert at Paisley Park on 31 December, raising money for the Minnesota Coalition for the Homeless. Implicitly approving his band's credentials, jazz legend Miles Davis guested during the encore. The pair had attempted a collaboration in 1986, when Prince offered – then withdrew – the track 'Can I Play With U?', intended for Davis's first Warner Bros album, *Tutu*. Now, with Paisley Park enabling him to record music uninterrupted, at a greater rate than ever before, yet another scrapped project would lead Prince to a grand artistic statement – but not before a spiritual crisis showed him the way.

6

God: Sexy?

'**D**ON'T BUY THE BLACK ALBUM. I'M SORRY.' Some fans failed to notice it – both the plea and *The Black Album* itself. The message briefly emerged from the jumble of letters swimming across the 'Alphabet St.' promo video. *The Black Album*, however, didn't officially hit the shelves, but it quickly became the biggest-selling bootleg album of all time.

The Black Album had its roots in a then-unreleased *Camille* track, 'Rockhard in a Funky Place', as well as some oversexed party tunes recorded for Sheila E.'s December 1986 birthday bash – songs put together for fun, not necessarily for release. 'It was never intended to be an album,' Susan Rogers says. 'We just wanted stuff to dance to at the party.' But, stung by criticism that he was losing his Black audience, Prince had an 'I'll-show-them moment', strung the songs together and presented the collection to Warner Bros for release in December 1987, with a plain black cover identifiable only by a peach catalogue number on the spine – no title, no credited artist. But then Prince blocked its release with no explanation, forcing Warner Bros to pull all 500,000 units they'd pressed. It cost him millions of dollars.

He felt 'remorse' about the album, Susan Rogers says. He'd made '*pro*active' records up to that point; *The Black*

Album was 'reactive', so 'he yanked it off the loading dock'. The story also began to circulate that Prince had experimented with ecstasy while spending an evening at Paisley Park with the young poet Ingrid Chavez, and became convinced that *The Black Album* was evil – he described seeing a vision of the word 'God' floating above him in a field. By February 1988, he'd recorded a loved-up corrective: *Lovesexy*.

In contrast to *The Black Album*'s skeletal funk, *Lovesexy* was a dense, at times impenetrable album whose positive message had to fight from underneath layers of production and an array of sonic tricks vying for attention. Songs like 'I Wish U Heaven' and 'Anna Stesia' found him again genuflecting before God, while 'Dance On' and 'Positivity' railed against social ills. A sensual hymn to the melting together of minds and bodies, 'When 2 R in Love' survived from *The Black Album*, while 'Eye No', 'Alphabet St.' and 'Lovesexy' sought to express his new enlightenment. After years of striving to harmonize the two, Prince had finally envisioned a state in which his sexual and spiritual impulses could be at one: 'lovesexy'. 'There's some really great stuff on the album,' Marylou Badeaux says, but without defining the concept, 'people were confused'.

Noting that 'the hardest questions may not lend themselves to easy answers, but make for much better music', *Rolling Stone* happily followed where Prince led. Shot by Jean-Baptiste Mondino, Prince's original choice of director for *Under the Cherry Moon*, *Lovesexy*'s album cover – picturing him reclining on a floral arrangement, in reference to Botticelli's *The Birth of Venus*, as if reborn himself, with a strategically placed stamen rising next to him – caused major chains like Walmart to refuse to stock it.

Meanwhile, believing that his latest masterpiece should be experienced in full, as 'a mind trip, like a psychedelic movie', Prince insisted that the album be pressed as a forty-five-minute single-track movement that defied attempts to skip to favourite songs ('It was *all* we could do to talk him into allowing us to give radio a banded version,' Badeaux says). Also, there were no promo videos – until slipping sales figures changed his mind. But though 'Alphabet St.' made it to No. 8 on the *Billboard* Hot 100 (No. 3 on the Hot Black Singles chart), 'Glam Slam' and 'I Wish You Heaven' failed to reach the Hot 100 at all, with 'Glam Slam' even stalling outside the Hot Black Singles Top 40. The album itself landed just outside the pop Top 10, Prince's worst chart performance since *Controversy*.

With a more positive reception in the UK and Europe (a string of Top 5 placements, including his first No. 1 album in the UK), Prince launched his *Lovesexy* tour in France, on 8 July. A high-concept show, even by his standards, it cemented his place as the greatest live performer in the world as he staged a battle between good and evil, symbolically killing his licentious persona at the end of each night's first half – which included songs such as 'Erotic City', 'Head' and *Black Album* tracks 'Bob George' and 'Superfunkycalifragisexy' – before performing a more spiritually minded set of hits and *Lovesexy* songs.

To help realize his vision for the show, held in the round, with the band performing in the middle of the arena – itself a rarity for live performances at the time – Prince asked

Roy Bennett for a stage design that included a swing set, a miniature basketball court and a three-quarter-sized replica of his 1967 Thunderbird, complete with unnecessary modifications: working lights, windscreen wipers, power windows and a removable roof. 'There was more to it than we actually ended up having,' Bennett says of the overall design – including waterfalls that ran off the side of the stage, and a telescoping fountain that, during its inaugural test run outside Paisley Park, shot water everywhere.

'Prince spent a shitload of money, and you could not stop him,' Bennett says. 'He did not want to know what things cost, he just wanted it to happen.' This time, he had no choice but to tour the US in order to recoup the costs. But with a three-year gap between the *Purple Rain* and *Lovesexy* tours, 'America had already moved on': many nights found Prince performing to partially filled venues. With a growing payroll and the mounting costs of storing and transporting all the equipment, a tour that should have been a guaranteed money-maker severely depleted his finances. 'We had a big graph,' manager Bob Cavallo later recalled. 'I put it on an easel showing the decline in revenue and increase in spending. He just walked and turned it over.'

When Prince realized how much he'd spent, he'd blame someone else – often management. 'Steven Fargnoli loved Prince. He did everything he could for him, and he took so much abuse,' Bennett says. Exasperated, Cavallo, Ruffalo & Fargnoli began to pull away. On 31 December 1988, with a string of Japanese tour dates still to complete in February, Prince fired them, losing the longest-standing supporters of his entire career – a team that had helped take him from cult-level artist to global megastar.

* * * * *

Prince needed a saviour, and there was no shortage of self-appointed heroes. 'Everybody thought they could save' him, Roy Bennett says. Unwilling to deal with the 'rotating door of clowns' that began cycling through Paisley Park, however, Prince tried to convince Bennett to liaise with them. Soon the designer found himself being blamed for Prince's spending. 'I said, "See if you can control him." Of course, they felt the wrath of Prince when they tried.'

First up was Albert Magnoli ('A nice guy, but definitely not cut out to be a manager. It was beyond him'). Prince sought to use the *Purple Rain* director's leverage in Hollywood to get backing for a sequel to the film that had boosted both their careers. While struggling through scripts and casting, however, a new movie franchise was taking flight – one that Prince would end up riding to his greatest commercial heights since making his own cinematic breakthrough.

Director Tim Burton had used '1999' and 'Baby I'm a Star' in edits of his big-screen adaptation of *Batman* and intended to ask Prince to record new versions for use in the film. After watching a rough cut, Prince, who had learned to play the *Batman* TV theme as a child, recorded an album's worth of material. Prioritizing it over another new album, *Rave Unto the Joy Fantastic*, then taking shape in Paisley Park, and initially planning to cancel the Japanese *Lovesexy* shows – at a risk of being sued up to $20 million, a financial disaster he was eventually persuaded away from – Prince immersed himself in the project throughout February and March 1989.

Writing from the differing psychological perspectives of the movie's main characters – Bruce Wayne/Batman, The Joker and Vicki Vale – and deep into an intense affair with its female lead, Kim Basinger, Prince used the fictional characters to explore aspects of his own psyche, creating his own new persona in the process: the half-Batman, half-Joker alter ego Gemini, unleashed to run amok in the 'Batdance' and (as a half-Prince, half-Joker variant) 'Partyman' videos. Heavy on the bottom end – almost to the point of hinting at industrial music – the soundtrack album featured more songs than Burton could use in his film. However, with *Rolling Stone* calling it 'the biggest tie-in since shoelaces' and the *Detroit Free Press* exclaiming 'Holy hit singles, Batman! Prince has done it again!', *Batman* topped the Top Pop Albums chart and went to No. 5 in the Top Black Albums chart.

With Prince's best sales figures since *Purple Rain*, and a return to relevance on the silver screen, Magnoli convinced Warner Bros to take another original Prince film seriously. ('There was always hope that he can rally,' Bob Merlis says.) Conceptually, *Graffiti Bridge* – named after a local Minneapolis landmark – had been taking shape since September 1987, and revisited the conflict between The Kid and The Time. Prince's original choice of female lead, Madonna, a fellow winner at the 1987 Golden Raspberry Awards (for her role in *Shanghai Surprise*), hadn't been convinced by his original script – a twenty-page treatment kept well away from outside screenwriters – but with Kim Basinger having relocated to Minneapolis, he had a new female lead and a new script, along with a new film division, Paisley Park Films, launched with Albert Magnoli.

Magnoli envisioned a high-budget production, but Prince wanted to shoot on the Paisley Park soundstage, with the aim of rushing the film out within the year. Parting ways with Magnoli, he hired Arnold Stiefel and Randy Phillips – who 'had their own agenda', says Roy Bennett – to a twelve-month contract, on the assurance that they would get the movie made.

The new team secured Warner Bros Pictures's financial backing, with the proviso that Prince deliver the original line-up of The Time – Jimmy Jam and Terry Lewis included. Banking on another box-office smash, they wanted in. Having secured his old rivals, however, Prince lost his female lead when Kim Basinger refused to put up with his philandering. 'She went out of town,' Marylou Badeaux says, 'and she rang him later in the day and there was already another woman there.'

Without scriptwriters, directors or acting coaches, Prince and his latest band, plus new love interest Ingrid Chavez (as female lead Aura), The Time and cameo spots from Jill Jones and musical legends like George Clinton and Mavis Staples, failed to gel on a sterile set lacking clear leadership. 'There's professional level and there's college level,' Badeaux, who was present at much of the filming, says of Prince's directing style. 'You get one or two takes and that's it.'

Prince had promised The Time that this movie would tell their story, but any sense of plot, cohesion or quality control – along with a planned new Time album, *Corporate World* – soon began to fall away. 'A lot of the stuff that made the story make sense ended up on the cutting-room floor,' says Michael Bland, who had recently replaced Sheila E. as Prince's drummer. What remained was a battle between a self-pitying Kid and his hoodlum rivals over the fictional Glam Slam nightclub (a real-life equivalent was under construction in Minneapolis – one of four Glam Slam venues that would be financed by Prince throughout the 1990s), and an unclear spiritual message, tacked together with musical set pieces.

Having failed to complete the movie in time for a scheduled tour, Prince edited the footage on VHS tapes during downtime in hotels, phoning changes through to Steven Rivkin, brother of Bobby Z., in the editing suite. On days off, he flew back to call the shots in person. Premiered in November 1990, the finished movie was 'one of the purest, most spiritual, uplifting things I've ever done', Prince later reflected. Critics were less forgiving: *The Washington Post* felt it made *Under the Cherry Moon* look like Orson Welles's *Citizen Kane*, and 'might draw bigger crowds' at 'Hollywood's Hall of Shamelessness'.

Mixing Prince tracks with others sung by The Time, Mavis Staples, George Clinton and Tevin Campbell, the soundtrack album fared better, hitting No. 6 on both the Top Pop and Top Black Albums charts. Relying on reworked songs written as far back as 1981, alongside repurposed *Rave Unto the Joy Fantastic* material and the inspired collision of operatic vocals, Middle Eastern motifs and speaker-rattling beats that made up 'Thieves in the Temple' – the only truly new song from the era, originally written in response to Kim Basinger's desertion – it was praised as the 'creative and commercially successful master stroke' the film wasn't.

If the eventual Time album that emerged alongside it, *Pandemonium* – named after the club that Morris Day owned in the movie – sometimes matched its title, the record's high points, also exhumed from The Vault, offered an early 1990s update on their patented funk. They also drew a line under The Time's studio work with Prince. The group would tour sporadically in the decades that followed, opening for Prince on occasion; they returned to the studio in 2011, releasing the album *Condensate* as The Original 7ven.

Graffiti Bridge was in the red (Warner Bros Pictures's $7 million investment recouped just $4.2 million at the box office), while Prince had been on the road, trying to stay in the black with a cost-cutting stage set that kept overheads low. Launched on 2 June, his new band – guitarist Miko Weaver, bassist Levi Seacer, Jr., keyboardist Dr. Fink and drummer Michael Bland were joined by keyboardist/vocalist Rosie Gaines and a trio of dancers who had cameoed in *Purple Rain*, Tony Mosley, Damon Dickson and Kirk Johnson, known as The Game Boyz – took the *Nude* tour through to September, again favouring the UK, Europe and Japan, and including a record-breaking sixteen-night run at London's Wembley Arena.

Meanwhile, the *Graffiti Bridge* edits weren't the only video tapes that kept Prince awake in his hotel room. Enthused by the Arabic strains of 'Thieves in the Temple',

Janelle Garcia, the mother of Mayte Garcia, a sixteen-year-old professional belly dancer of Puerto Rican descent, convinced her daughter to get a showreel to Prince (a young Mayte had already received national exposure, at the age of eight, on the TV talent show *That's Incredible!*).

'I kept it very simple,' Mayte says of the video. 'I put in me dancing with a sword and doing a drum solo, and then I wrote a letter and taped a picture to it.' Her father, a military pilot, was stationed with his family in Wiesbaden, Germany; on 8 August, Mayte's mother and sister accompanied her to nearby Mannheim for that night's show. As Prince's tour bus pulled into the Maimarkthalle venue, he caught a glimpse of the young dancer waiting for him, telling Rosie Gaines: 'There's my future wife.'

Inspired by her tape, and the music she set her routines to, Prince began a long-distance courtship with Mayte, developed over letters and late-night phone calls, while occasionally flying her out to visit him on tour. 'The environment that Prince had was very professional' and 'majestic', Mayte recalls. 'He would ask permission to hang out … We'd talk about movies; I would say that I'm doing a show and tell him something funny that happened.' Feeling that 'there was an innocence to it that he really took to', Mayte soon found herself receiving new, Arabic-inspired music in the post. 'I didn't even think that it was written for me, but he would say, "Can you dance to it?"' Thinking she might be asked to appear in a music video, Mayte responded with footage of her performing to his new songs. 'The penny never dropped,' she says. 'I just started sending what he asked for.'

Another dancer had also caught Prince's attention. During the *Purple Rain* era, he told Susan Rogers, 'The future of music is going to be bass and drums, with vocals over the top.' Now that future had arrived. His previous engagement with hip-hop had been 'Dead on It', a disparaging *Black Album* track that claimed the only good rapper was a dead one. After hearing Tony Mosley (now going as Tony M.) rap during a soundcheck, however, Prince saw a way of integrating hip-hop into his music and gave the Game Boy a solo spot during performances of the *Batman* track 'The Future'.

'Kids save a lot of money for a long time to buy tickets, and I like to give them what they want,' he asserted. The tour's reliance on a hits-stuffed setlist also ensured that fair-weather concertgoers, less interested in his new music than they were the songs they already knew, got what they came for – and not for the last time. For some fans, however, the hip-hop concessions foreshadowed a divisive new direction his music would take. 'Everything kind of lost its plot,' says Roy Bennett, one of the few people who remained from Prince's breakthrough years. 'It was going all over the place and the car was a little out of control. I did my best to keep things focused.'

7

Symbol o' the Times

With his career in a tailspin, Prince had discussions with Warner Bros heads Mo Ostin and Lenny Waronker about his next album, *Diamonds and Pearls*. 'The implication was: "Look, this is really important. You've gotta turn this around,"' says Jeff Gold, who, as Warner Bros's Senior Vice President of Creative Services, was about to start working with Prince on a pioneering holographic design for the album cover. 'I don't think anybody was telling Prince what to do, but making suggestions that he was open to, which was an unusual situation.'

Prince was also spending time in the clubs, seeing what kinds of songs filled the dancefloor, and then recording his own takes on them, built, like hip-hop, on samples, but largely using his own new music for source material. He invited journalists from trendsetting magazines such as *Spin* to studio playbacks to gauge their reactions. 'He had the insight to know that he was too old to flex himself in the hip-hop game,' says drummer Michael Bland, who had been recording new material with Prince on the *Nude* tour. 'But he was in a position to mix that with actual instrumentation … It was an organic way to stay relevant without giving into the tropes and the trite production models of the time.'

'I wear what I wear because I don't like clothes,' Prince asserted.
While each band member developed their own individual styles for Prince's first tour,
of 1979–80, Prince conceived his androgynous look as one of 'pure sexuality'.
L–R: Bassist André Cymone, Prince, guitarist Dez Dickerson.

While touring the *Dirty Mind* album, Prince encouraged his band to be as outrageous as possible. 'We wanted to shock people and just get attention,' says keyboardist Lisa Coleman. 'Even if it was bad attention – it didn't matter.'

TOP – As Prince's first successful side project, The Time 'represented a kind of Black culture that was more pure and more distilled than Prince's own cultural make-up', says studio engineer Susan Rogers. L–R: Frontman Morris Day, bassist Terry Lewis.

ABOVE – In masterminding Vanity 6's career, Prince 'opened up things for other female bands that came after us – the whole sexuality thing, if nothing else', says Brenda Bennett. L–R: Brenda Bennett, Denise Matthews (aka Vanity), Susan Moonsie.

Playing to sold-out arenas on the *Purple Rain* tour, Prince sought to make audiences feel as though they were in the movie. 'We were just on another planet,' says set designer Roy Bennett. 'When you have an arena full of women screaming, there's no sound in the world like that anywhere.'

Replacing the 'raw animal magnetism' of Vanity with what Brenda Bennett calls 'more of the homey, pretty-girl-next-door quality', Patricia Kotero was rechristened Apollonia and given the lead female role in *Purple Rain*.

Prince expanded The Revolution's line-up for his *Parade* shows of 1986, while continuing to push his own performances to the limit. 'Sometimes, after gigs, he'd be on the floor and they'd be giving him oxygen,' says Lisa Coleman. 'It was like being an athlete.'

After disbanding The Revolution, Prince released the *Sign o' the Times* album in 1987, crediting it solely to himself. 'It was like breaking up with my boyfriend. I felt really sad and heartbroken,' says Lisa Coleman.

TOP – For his ambitious *Lovesexy* tour, Prince's stage set included a miniature basketball court and a three-quarter-sized replica of his 1967 Thunderbird. 'Prince spent a shitload of money, and you could not stop him,' says Roy Bennett. L–R: Dancer Cat Glover, Prince.

ABOVE – Though Prince called the *Graffiti Bridge* movie 'one of the purest, most spiritual, uplifting things I've ever done', it failed to reach the heights of *Purple Rain*. L–R: Female lead Ingrid Chavez, as Aura; Prince as The Kid.

When forming The New Power Generation for his 1991 album,
Diamonds and Pearls, Prince wanted a 'more ethnocentric' presentation,
says drummer Michael Bland. L–R: Guitarist Levi Seacer, Jr, singer/keyboardist
Rosie Gaines, Prince, The Game Boyz (Damon Dickson, Kirk Johnson, Tony M.).

Prince met belly dancer Mayte Garcia in 1990, when she was sixteen. By the time he set out on the *Act II* tour, in 1993, she had become one of the biggest influences on his music. 'We evolved and just understood each other on a whole other level,' Mayte says.

While fighting with Warner Bros over his rights as an artist,
Prince launched his own NPG stores in Minneapolis and London, selling his
music and other merchandise direct to fans without the help of a record label.
'He was a total visionary,' says former Warner Bros exec Jeff Gold.

After a relatively quiet period in the early 2000s, Prince made
a headline-grabbing return to the mainstream when he opened
the 2004 Grammys with Beyoncé. 'Don't hate us 'cause we fabulous,'
he teased the audience.

Prince married his second wife, Manuela Testolini, on New Year's Eve 2001. 'She was a huge fan and she really enjoyed him both as an artist and a person. But she also saw the bullshit,' says former Paisley Park studio engineer Hans-Martin Buff.

Prince's landmark performance at Super Bowl XLI, in 2007, went down as
the greatest halftime show in history. Despite an unexpected storm jeopardizing
the event, Prince had one request: 'Can you make it rain *harder*?'

TOP – Prince used his *Welcome 2 America* tour of 2010–11 as a way of raising money for charities and other organizations, including New York City's American Ballet Theatre, which appointed Misty Copeland as their first Black female principal dancer.

ABOVE – With the all-female power trio 3rdEyeGirl, Prince unleashed heavy funk-rock performances in small venues, receiving praise for being 'a galaxy-class showman playing like a band with a residency in a local bar'. L–R: Guitarist Donna Grantis, Prince, bassist Ida Nielsen.

Prince's new band, almost all handpicked from the Minneapolis scene, would help the transition – and would be named, portentously, The New Power Generation, after a phrase that had appeared at the start of the *Lovesexy* album. Sonny Thompson (now Sonny T.), who had mentored the young Prince in Minneapolis, took over on bass, as Levi Seacer, Jr., replaced a departing Miko Weaver on guitar. Rosie Gaines resumed her roles as a singer and keyboardist, while Tony M. was given more prominence as a full-time rapper. Tommy Barbarella (formerly Tommy Elm), the only white member of the group, replaced Matt Fink, the last remaining member of Prince's original band, as second keyboardist. 'The whole presentation was a bit more ethnocentric,' says Michael Bland, 'and that might have turned some people off. But to fans of real Black music – that turned a lot of people on.'

A mix of young, ambitious newcomers and seasoned professionals, The NPG worked up an earthier, more organic sound that complemented Prince's new direction. 'He used that band to its full extent,' says Barbarella, who sometimes found himself 'hanging on for dear life … frankly scared shitless'. New songs were worked up during soundchecks – sometimes Prince's ideas, sometimes a groove the band kicked into; recording sessions would yield several songs a night, each captured in just one or two takes. 'We could play anything he thought of,' Barbarella says. 'He would make up crazy lines and bizarre transitions, and we could pull it off.'

* * * * *

It had been over a year since *Graffiti Bridge*, and yet another management shake-up had distracted from getting the music out there. Looking to further widen the gap between new albums, Warner Bros suggested consolidating Prince's position as the 1980s' greatest hitmaker with a greatest-hits set, sending Prince into overdrive to prove that *Diamonds and Pearls* had enough hits of its own. Ignoring budget restrictions in the pursuit of MTV placement – and to fulfil his ambition of creating a small-screen take on the 1979 historical epic *Caligula* – the 'Gett Off' promo video alone cost over five times more than the $200,000 earmarked for the shoot.

Accompanied, in all public appearances, by the looka-like female dancers Diamond (Lori Elle) and Pearl (Robia LaMorte), Prince had dropped complex artistic statements in favour of projecting ostentatious success. In his deter-mination to reassert himself on the charts, he doubled down on *Diamonds and Pearls*'s production: 'You know when you would buy someone's record and there's always an element missing? The voice is wrong or the drums are lame or something? On mine there's nothing missing,' he boasted to *Details* magazine.

With its dense R&B sound meticulously crafted to attract radio play, however, *Diamonds and Pearls* succeeded where Prince's overproduced debut album had not. Buoyed by all the promotional activity, it shot to No. 1 on the *Billboard* Top R&B Albums chart, outperforming its *Billboard* 200 Top Albums peak by two places. If 'Gett Off' and 'Cream' were camp, rather than provocative ('He kind of cleaned up his act,' Michael Bland says. 'He stopped being so lascivious and it got to be more about the music'), that only further encouraged airplay.

The title track, meanwhile, soared with Rosie Gaines's supporting gospel-tinged vocals. Ceding verses to Tony M. on almost half the album's songs, however, didn't convince everybody. 'I was dismayed that Prince wanted to emulate the sound of current Black music,' Paisley Park engineer Michael Koppelman recalled. 'It was really frustrating to see what I consider to be a very talented musician fucking around with a lot of trendy crap.'

Commercially, however, *Diamonds and Pearls* 'was a comeback for him, to some pop relevance', Tommy Barbarella says. 'He had some hits and we were really in the mix of pop culture, Black music at that time ... A lot of that record, with the rap stuff on it, is still super creative and had never been done like that before.' Alan Leeds, however, noted the reluctance of 'the "keep it real" hip-hop community' to take seriously the gun-shaped microphone Prince would soon brandish in photos and promo videos ('My words of peace go in2 the gun and nullify its power,' Prince later explained).

Despite *Diamonds and Pearls*'s sales figures, some critics also felt Prince was chasing trends rather than setting them, with the *NME* hearing 'too much clutter and dead weight' in the songs, and *Entertainment Weekly* bemoaning the sound of an artist spending 'too much time in his hermetically sealed world'.

Audiences struggling with Prince's own hip-hop excursions were reluctant to embrace Tara Leigh Patrick, a cut-rate hip-hop Vanity who, as Carmen Electra, opened a run of shows on the *Diamonds and Pearls* tour before being dropped from the bill. The tour launched in April 1992 and, taking in Japan, Australia, Europe and the UK, Prince's band were once again augmented by The Game Boyz, their female counterparts, Diamond and Pearl, plus a DJ and a full brass section. Rounding out the expanded seventeen-piece line-up was Mayte, 'pointe-shoe me – an exotic person with coins all over herself'.

For the six months leading up to Mayte's eighteenth birthday, Prince had been given power of attorney over her, enabling the dancer to fly out to Paisley Park for recording sessions and video shoots. 'He promised my father that he would protect me,' Mayte says. 'I remember having a bodyguard from the get-go.' Now performing on stage during select songs, at least one band member wondered aloud, 'I don't even understand what she's doing here,' while it was intimated that others should not even look at her. Before one show, Chris Poole, Prince's UK press agent, witnessed Prince privately serenading Mayte, who was draped on the top of his piano, with a rendition of 'Somewhere Over the Rainbow'. 'It was a sort of *Fabulous Baker Boys* moment,' Poole says. 'It was beautiful.'

Beautiful – and at odds with the excess of the tour itself: retina-scorching lighting, foliage, oversized female statues and an large accessory, shaped like merged Venus and Mars symbols, hanging from the ceiling. Between shows, the band crammed into one bus while thirteen lorries took the gear to the next venue; Prince travelled in his own specially decked-out bus. 'It was mainly a bed,' Chris Poole recalls. 'A couple of chairs and a gigantic bed, done out with floaty stuff and candles.' Unplanned stops might signal a 'hasty reshuffle' of the travel arrangements, with dancers Diamond and Pearl being relegated to the band bus, and Mayte called aboard to travel with Prince.

In contrast to the fiscal restraint of the *Nude* shows, the *Diamonds and Pearls* tour was another financial drain. Meanwhile, Prince also gave fans a glimpse of the follow-up album he'd almost completed, slipping 'Sexy M.F.' into the setlist ahead of its single release. Prince had good reason to rush new music into the stores. With *Diamonds and Pearls* going platinum, selling more than any of his albums since *Purple Rain*, he leveraged a new contract with Warner Bros.

Keen to encourage him to continue recording commercially minded material, the label offered terms that included a Vice President title within the company's A&R division, a new royalty rate and a hefty advance of $10 million an album – provided that its predecessor sold over five million copies. With the ink barely dry, Prince issued a press release celebrating this new, unprecedented '$100 million' deal – a significant increase on the $60 million contracts that Madonna and Michael Jackson had recently signed. It was 'a lie', Bob Merlis says. 'If every term is met and he sells all the records and there's an escalation of royalties, it's potentially $100 million.' Warner Bros hadn't written him a cheque for that amount, but neither could they go public with the real terms of their agreement, with its advance of 'probably $30 million'.

* * * * *

A stack of Arabic CDs sat in Prince's studio as he mined them for samples to build new songs around. Meanwhile, postponing her plans to continue training in Cairo, Mayte was installed nearby in a rented apartment and left to anticipate his calls ('I have a letter where he says "good things come to those who wait",' she says). Since meeting two years before, Prince's infatuation had developed into fascination. He took an increasing interest in the Egyptian culture that informed Mayte's belly dancing, and began to believe they had been fated to meet.

Under amateur hypnosis sessions that were 'a form of meditation', the pair would 'take ourselves into a different level of consciousness where pure complete love was coming', Mayte says – sharing details about her past life as Princess Mayte of Cairo; her desires for a family; the ways their souls had met, and would continue to do so, over centuries. 'We evolved and just understood each other on a whole other level.' Although Mayte resisted his efforts to rename her Arabia, she had become central to Prince's new album, influencing his music in profound ways.

Released in October 1992, the record was given an unconventional name: a glyph that mixed the male and female astrological signs with the alchemical symbol for soapstone. Dubbed 'Love Symbol', its title was impossible to pronounce – and the album itself not much easier to comprehend. A seventy-five-minute 'rock soap opera', it purported to tell the story of Prince's relationship with the Crown Princess of Cairo, and their attempts to evade assassins out to steal the 'Three Chains of Turin'. Of a number of dramatic segues that held the plot together on early versions of the album, only two remained by the time the record hit the shelves, as Prince altered the tracklist to make way for a new song, 'Eye Wanna Melt With U'.

What Prince lost in narrative clarity he gained in a club-focused track whose intensity reflected his all-consuming thoughts of Mayte, placing it in the middle of an album that cycled through jazz, funk, R&B, reggae and even classical music, and assimilated hip-hop with confidence on the opening 'My Name is Prince'. But the true apogee of his obsessions became clear on '7', a mix of Middle Eastern instrumentation and acoustic guitar built around a sample of Lowell Fulson's 1967 R&B cut 'Tramp', in which Prince battles the seven deadly sins in order to unite with a love that transcends space and time. The song's promo video portrayed the sins as seven incarnations of Prince himself, while he and Mayte were surrounded by a troupe of children dressed to look like them. The penny dropped. 'That's when it was like, OK, I get it now,' Mayte says. After the shoot, Prince suggested she start taking birth control.

Effortlessly creative where *Diamonds and Pearls*'s precision felt hard-earned, 'Love Symbol' was 'the record where we really felt like a band', says Tommy Barbarella. 'Almost everything was recorded live and then he would overdub on it ... He didn't want you to perfect it or change it. He liked the live feel.' *Rolling Stone* praised the album's 'wonderfully hyped-up take on Seventies funk' that captured 'the glory days of James Brown and The JB's', even if its wider ambitions left 'a high-concept muddle' whose sales figures fell four million short of their five million target.

The *Act I* tour, which ran throughout March and April 1993, brought the album's storyline to life. As his first US trek in five years, Prince led The New Power Generation – minus Rosie Gaines, who had defected to Motown after the *Diamonds and Pearls* tour – Mayte and The Game Boyz through a 'Love Symbol'-focused set, before performing a hits-filled second half.

By the time *Act II* came to the UK and Europe in the summer, the setlist was given over to hits, but Prince continued to seek new avenues for his music, announcing his intention to pursue 'alternative media projects, including live theatre, interactive media, nightclubs and motion pictures'. 'He was very interested in theatre,' Mayte says. 'He didn't want to just be a "rock star".' After the Joffrey Ballet staged a production to his music, he and Mayte started NPG Dance Company. 'He was like, "They did so well, but it was just one content of classical ballet. Why can't there be hip-hop dancers and jazz dancers and flamenco dancers and belly dancers?" That was something he wanted to conquer.'

March and April had been spent recording songs for a movie musical, *I'll Do Anything*, that tested so poorly it was reworked into a straightforward comedy-drama that left Prince's songs in The Vault. In a gap between the *Act I* and *Act II* shows, Prince filmed a jam with Michael Bland and Sonny T., intercutting the footage with scenes shot with the actress Vanessa Marcil for a dramatized project called *The Undertaker*. And while the *Act II* tour closed, *Glam Slam Ulysses* opened in Prince's Los Angeles-based Glam Slam venue. With a storyline based on Homer's *Odyssey*, and Carmen Electra given another shot, it folded after a handful of performances and terrible reviews.

The most dramatic event of Prince's career, however, came on 7 June 1993, his thirty-fifth birthday: Prince was no longer Prince. From now on he would take the Love Symbol as his name. Androgyny had long been central to his presentation, but this was a step beyond high heels, make-up and feminine clothing: in identifying as a glyph that combined the two gender signs, Prince signalled that his very essence fused the two. 'He really wanted to see this feminine quality,' Mitch Monson, one of the symbol's co-designers, told *Wired* magazine. 'He saw those elements being important, and being integrated.'

Prototypes of the symbol had already appeared earlier in his work – hidden in the *1999* album cover; painted on his *Purple Rain* motorbike – but this was more than an exercise in rebranding. While visiting Mayte and her family in Puerto Rico, in December 1992, he had had a new epiphany. 'We were sitting at the piano and he was like, "I'm gonna change my name,"' Mayte recalls, adding, 'He always told me he would have these revelations ... Something happened to him in Puerto Rico and he was very quiet about it. And I respected that.'

'I had searched deep within my heart and spirit, and I wanted to make a change and move to a new plateau in my life,' Prince told TV host Larry King in 1999. While some of the band were confused at the time ('Why can't it just be normal?' Tommy Barbarella thought. 'Can't we just focus on the music?'), the decision was 'deeply personal', says Michael Bland. 'I called him "Prince" one day in rehearsal and he turned around and he ice-grilled me. He said, "Don't call me Prince ever again. That's not my name anymore."'

For some of the staff at Warner Bros, it was an opportunity to have fun with what they thought was a cynical marketing ploy. 'People from his office would call and say, "I've got my boss on the phone,"' Jeff Gold recalls. 'And I'd go, "Who's that?" "You know, my boss." Or we'd call and say, "Is Prince there? I need to talk to Prince." Just pushing back – but it was good natured.'

The label also serviced the media with floppy discs containing the image, though journalists often settled for The Artist Formerly Known as Prince, or TAFKAP. Prince himself modified the nickname to The Artist while admitting that he had yet to 'hear a sound that will give me a feeling of what my name will sound like'. All he knew was that it was 'a representation of me and what my music is about'. He later revealed to Oprah Winfrey, 'Recent analysis has proved that there's probably two people inside of me.' He further explained to director Spike Lee: 'I was a little ashamed of what Prince had become. I really felt like a product.'

Product was what Warner Bros had in mind – and not a new album. 'The biggest disservice he did to himself was releasing music too quickly,' Marylou Badeaux says. Trying to stem the flow, the label declined to release The New Power Generation's debut album, *Goldnigga*, in favour of their long-planned hits collection. As they prepared the three-disc *The Hits/The B-Sides* for release that September, The Artist announced that the *Act II* shows would mark fans' last opportunity to hear those songs: they were Prince's, not his. Besides, a record label shouldn't be able to tell him what to do with his art. 'From now on, Warner only gets old songs out of the vault,' he told *Vibe* magazine. 'New songs we'll play at shows. Music should be free, anyway.'

Goldnigga 'was not a super commercial effort', Michael Bland says. 'You're taking the same ensemble that you used in presenting *Diamonds and Pearls*, and now it's like the darker side of that. It's very heavily hip-hop influenced.' Through frontman Tony M., Prince asserted Black masculinity across an album that had its own narrative structure, with a recurring 'Goldnigga' theme that conjured a 1970s Blaxploitation vibe. Ignoring the exclusivity of his contract with Warner Bros, he pressed *Goldnigga* on CD himself, selling it at *Act II* shows. 'He was always like, "If you don't want to help, that's fine. Just back up and give me room to do what I got to do,"' Michael Bland says.

The group performed support slots throughout August and September, setting the stage for Prince to expand on his grievances with Warner Bros's reluctance to release his new material – some of which was aired alongside the promised hits. With each set opening with Mayte, disguised in a military hat accessorized with gold chains that dangled in front of her face, miming to 'My Name is Prince', the real Prince further distanced himself from what he felt his past represented. 'London, my name is not Prince,' he told the audience during the tour's final show, at Wembley Arena. That same night, he was covered in a black shroud and carried off stage, as if to his own interment.

8

The Hate Experience

'**P**rince is dead.' That chant would soon fill venues as the live-and-well Artist focused on performing his new material, some of which would be issued as New Power Generation side projects, some of which would be attributed to Prince, whose 'death' would be announced in Spanish on his reborn self's first album, *The Gold Experience.* Not that fans could hear it. A discussion with Mo Ostin had left Prince furious at the insinuation that Warner Bros owned his ideas. 'He was so hot you could have fried an egg on his forehead,' Michael Bland says.

He was also increasingly agitated over the label's ownership of his master tapes. 'During one meeting, he said, "I just can't believe Warner Bros won't give me my masters back,"' Jeff Gold recalls. 'And he had recently renegotiated his deal … If owning your masters is a priority, that's the time to talk about it.' In negotiations, however, leveraging higher royalty rates and advances had taken precedence over ownership of his master tapes. 'He totally wanted to have his cake and eat it, too.'

Warner Bros's own concerns were coming to a head: their star's relentless work rate had become 'a critical problem', says Bob Merlis. 'He wanted to put out multiple albums every year,' without giving the label enough time to maximize a record's sales before the next one came along. 'You need to tell them I need my music out more quickly,' Prince told Marylou Badeaux. 'Don't you understand? The music comes through me. I have no control.'

He made the label an offer: issue the new Prince album, *Come*, alongside *The Gold Experience*, on 7 June 1994 – a year to the day after his name change – and see which performed better. But Warner Bros refused to release two competing records by the same artist, no matter what names were on the covers. They'd also stopped bankrolling Paisley Park Records that February. In response, Prince launched his own imprint, NPG Records, and convinced the label to let him self-release his new single, 'The Most Beautiful Girl in the World'.

At a cost of $2 million of his own money, he manufactured and marketed the single while striking a distribution deal with the independent imprint Bellmark, owned by former Stax Records Vice President Al Bell. Released on Valentine's Day, 'The Most Beautiful Girl in the World' shot to No. 3 on the Hot 100 and No. 2 on the Hot R&B Singles charts, while becoming his first UK No. 1 and his best-selling single since 'Batdance'. 'He did that to prove to them that he doesn't need them, they need him,' Michael Bland says. 'These are the things that were involved with him finally saying, "I'm going my own way. Try and stop me."'

'Doing stuff like making a deal with Al Bell, or selling records out of his NPG music shop' – stores that he opened in Minneapolis and London, where he could sell everything from Love Symbol-branded candles to his own Get Wild perfume – 'he was doing all kinds of shit that are not in the spirit of being signed to a record label,' says Jeff Gold.

An attempt to give *The Undertaker* audio recordings away as a free CD with *Guitar World* magazine was scuppered when the pressing plant asked Warner Bros why they'd received instructions to manufacture an album that wasn't on the schedule. The label 'called to gently remind him: "You can't just release whatever you want without talking to us first,"' Michael Bland says. Agitating to be freed from his contract, The Artist claimed that they didn't own his work: they had signed Prince, not him.

There was 'a logic behind it', says his UK publicist Chris Poole. 'He wasn't remotely mad. He knew exactly what he was doing, but I think he had some strange advice.' Warner Bros, however, felt he was being disingenuous: 'I can't believe he actually thought he could get out of his deal because we had "Prince" signed,' says Jeff Gold.

Attempting to embarrass Warner Bros into action, Prince claimed they were refusing to release his new album, *The Gold Experience*, so the record that included 'The Most Beautiful Girl in the World' would never see the light of day. While also holding back two upbeat, guitar-based tracks, 'Endorphinmachine' and 'Dolphin', he kept the hit for himself and delivered a reworked *Come* to the label. With songs addressing child abuse ('Papa') and racism ('Race') alongside intense voyeuristic bondage fantasies ('Pheromone') and soundscapes devoted to achieving orgasm, the album swung from laidback R&B to frenetic early 1990s dance tracks that were a more comfortable fit than some of Prince's hip-hop excursions.

Come's artistic merits were, however, overshadowed by the circus surrounding its eventual release. It 'was obviously just – throw it together, give it to them so I'm outta here', Marylou Badeaux says. 'It's a piece of garbage.' Nevertheless, Warner Bros agreed to issue the album in August, credited to Prince, who posed before Gaudí's iconic La Sagrada Família on the cover, his birth and 'death' dates – 1958 and 1993 – printed either side of him.

While promoting the record, Warner Bros took out an advert in *Billboard* – a playful mix of symbols and text claiming that the label treated their artists with a lot of heart, whatever they wanted to be called; Warner just wanted to make money and 'have a good time'. 'So here's the new Prince album,' it concluded, before adding, 'But don't call him Prince.'

They had drawn 'first blood', Michael Bland says. 'At that point it escalated to a sort of public war.' Releasing an NPG Records sampler album that same week – *1-800-NEW-FUNK*, named after the freephone number through which Prince also sold records and merchandise ('I used to answer the phones,' Mayte says. 'He answered the phones sometimes, in this little Minnesota accent, and people wouldn't even know it'), and featuring new tracks by artists such as Mayte, The NPG and a rebooted Madhouse, plus George Clinton, Mavis Staples and Marvin Gaye's daughter, Nona – Prince took out a rival advert: 'We here at NPG Records treat our artists with *respect*,' it asserted. If its artists were sad, the label was sad; NPG Records just wanted to release music 'so u can have a good time'.

Trying to negotiate himself out of his Warner Bros contract, Prince also had to navigate himself back into solvency. Where most artists relied on revenue from concert tickets and merchandise to bolster record sales, his refusal to embark on large-scale tours, often avoiding the US entirely, missed several opportunities to maximize income. At a meeting for the *Come* album, he'd turned to Jeff Gold and said, 'Make this album big. I need the money.' ('It was the *only* vulnerable thing he ever said to me, *ever*,' Gold recalls.)

Increasingly erratic sales figures (*Come* had hit No. 15 in the US, his lowest placement since *Controversy*) were exacerbated by the sheer volume of music being released, while Paisley Park had become a critical drain on resources. Full-time catering and tailoring staff were on the payroll alongside his road crew and band. Instead of renting the studios and soundstage out to other artists during downtime, Prince had the facilities manned around the clock for personal use.

Meanwhile, overheads from running his NPG stores and Glam Slam clubs, along with mounting debts owed to filmmakers who had helped shoot his costly promo videos, and the cane-makers who manufactured bespoke fashion accessories, were taking their toll. 'He was always recording and he was always shooting video and he was always doing photo shoots,' Jeff Gold says. 'It was *really* clear that he was spending an *insane* amount of money … He would shoot these incredible set-ups and then try and reverse-engineer them into things.'

Many of these projects went into The Vault, never to be released. A January 1995 report by the *St. Paul Pioneer Press* exposed a dire situation in Minneapolis: 'Paisley Park Enterprises, the company that oversees most of Prince's business interests, is not paying its bills on time or at all.'

In an attempt to shore up cash, Prince finally allowed Warner Bros to release *The Black Album* – to a muted response that failed to see what all the fuss was about now the bounds of permissibility had been pushed beyond where he had left them in the late 1980s. It sounded quaint compared to the inflammatory gangsta rap pioneered by artists like N.W.A, its former members turned solo stars Ice Cube and Dr. Dre, and descendants the likes of Snoop Dogg. Prince had his publicist Karen Lee spread the story that he was 'thoroughly pissed off about' the album's release, and that he still didn't want it out there.

'This Warner Bros thing was really on him,' Michael Bland says. 'There were a lot of dark days.' Financial stresses were exacerbated by personnel issues at Paisley Park, with long-term employees moving on. A swathe of redundancies followed. Described by one staffer as 'arbitrary', they further reduced payroll and left Paisley Park running on a skeleton crew. 'He cleaned house – big time,' Tommy Barbarella says.

The following month, with Prince overseas at the European MTV Awards, guitarist Levi Seacer, Jr., who had been appointed president of NPG Records, absconded. 'He knew that Prince would try to keep him there, and he waited till we left town,' Michael Bland says. 'We came back … and he was gone. Changed his number. We didn't know if he was still in town or had moved. It was years before I got to speak to Levi again.'

'It was the worst period of my life,' Prince later confessed to Salon.com. 'I was being made physically ill by what was going on.' One day he turned up to rehearsals with 'slave' written on his cheek. 'Nobody asked him' about it, Michael Bland says. 'No questions.'

In public, Prince demanded full control of his master recordings. 'If you don't own your masters, your master owns you,' he told *Rolling Stone*, underscoring what he began to feel was unjust treatment at the hands of the record label. His '$100 million deal', he decided, had been Warner Bros's attempt to 'lock him into institutionalized slavery'. ('If $100 million makes you a slave, sign me up for it,' Bob Merlis says. 'That's very lucrative servitude.')

'It was just more crazy shit … yet another thing on the continuum,' says Jeff Gold. Despite arriving at Warner Bros's head office wearing the 'slave' make-up, meetings were conducted amicably. 'At no point was there any personal antagonism with anybody at Warner Bros that I knew about. He was arguing his case in the court of public opinion.'

Marylou Badeaux, who had championed Prince since he joined the label, surviving a string of personnel changes that left her as one of his only allies from the early days, 'wasn't thrilled about what he did', but accepted that 'it was his way of projecting what he had to say'. Although some staff took it personally, she understood that it wasn't about Warner Bros, it was about the way the music business as a whole was structured. 'He's trying to say: "You can't own me. You can't own my music. And as long as you tell me that that's what it is, then I am your slave." … Look what he's done for artists in general by making that stand.'

Any progressive points Prince had were, however, in danger of being overshadowed by what *Rolling Stone* called 'the most spectacular slow-motion career derailment in the history of popular music'. Under a new pseudonym, Tora Tora, he recorded the second New Power Generation album, *Exodus*. With Tony M. and The Game Boyz no longer in the fold, bassist Sonny T. became Prince's mouthpiece for further railings against the industry. 'He was like, "Sonny, you're the lead singer on this record. I can't say some of these things because they'll come for me,"' Michael Bland says.

An overlong jumble that featured individual moments of stand-out P-Funk-indebted music ('Get Wild', 'The Return of the Bump Squad') amid a messy narrative involving Sonny T. being spiked with some hallucinogenic soup, *Exodus* also included a visionary comment about downloading music. Dedicating the album 'to the memory of His Royal Badness', Prince wrapped his face in a scarf for public appearances with the band, but his bigger priority remained his own unreleased album, *The Gold Experience*.

While Warner Bros told the press that he had backed out of deals that would have led to its release, NPG Records printed flyers and posted messages on the internet that read 'Release Date: Never!', encouraging fans to petition the label to liberate the album. On the twenty-date *The Ultimate Live Experience* tour, in which a pared-back NPG – with Morris Hayes completing a double-keyboard line-up alongside Tommy Barbarella, Sonny T., Michael Bland and Mayte – took in the UK, Ireland, Belgium and the Netherlands in March 1995, Prince told attendees to record the shows. They would, he claimed, mark the only time the album's songs would be heard in public.

Much of the tour's elaborate stage set also remained locked away. Christened the 'Endorphinmachine', it featured a womb-like space with red curtains in the centre of the stage, where Prince housed the mixing board – and sometimes mixed the sound himself, causing issues for the band and the audience – a conveyer belt that took him to the front, and an elevator that looked like a phallus. 'It's artistic, but it's genitalia,' Michael Bland says. It was also built without any consideration towards travel: 'This monstrosity has no right angles. It's got no hinges. There's no way to really break it down.'

Some parts got damaged en route to Wembley Arena; a gold bed, with an angel for a headboard, ended up being too heavy for the stage, so was left behind in London. Other portions of the set were deposited around the country as the tour continued ('He ended up with basically this pod thing in the middle of the stage,' Chris Poole says). Tommy Barbarella was given a new piece of equipment – a customized portable keyboard dubbed the PurpleAxxe, which Prince held the patent to, with light-up keys, lasers and a built-in smoke machine – but a stunt in which Barbarella swung across the stage in a harness while playing it was short-lived after he landed on his keyboards. 'I got "the look" like it was my fault,' Barbarella says. 'That may have been my last flight.'

The whole tour 'was one of those *Spinal Tap* moments where we really had to laugh about it, though we were kind of embarrassed', Michael Bland says. 'But we still whooped it.'

With Britpop and grunge holding sway in the UK, Prince faced partially full venues despite turning out blistering performances that suggested *The Gold Experience* truly did contain some of his most vibrant music in years. Nightly aftershows were staged to help shore up funds, but only the faithful were listening. Fans began anti-Warner Bros chants. 'Prince would turn around and look at us like, "Do you hear this?"' Michael Bland says. 'The people were with it … They knew something had to change. That Prince was on the right side of history.'

To the wider public, however, the name change and bitter disputes distracted from the one thing Prince always claimed he was about: music. When the media accused him of insensitivity surrounding his slavery comments, he shifted the focus away from Warner Bros and back to his art: 'When I started writing "slave" on my face, I did it because I had become a slave to myself,' he told the *St. Paul Pioneer Press*, adding, 'I felt like I was in a box spiritually, not creatively.'

When *The Gold Experience* finally saw the light of day, released jointly between NPG Records and Warner Bros on 26 September 1995, it revealed that The Artist's creativity hadn't died with Prince. Hailed by *Vibe* magazine as 'his best effort since the 90s almost happened without him', the album took in hip-hop/funk hybrids promoting female empowerment ('P. Control') while effortlessly flaunting his rock credentials alongside ballads that elevated themselves beyond earthly realms.

'Gold' delivered an attempt at a 1990s 'Purple Rain'; with more bluster and less cultural relevance, it fell shy of the mark, but closed a refreshingly direct collection of songs that cohered around a prescient concept guided by an 'NPG Operator' who presented the record as a series of interactive experiences chosen by the listener. But, having promoted it for the last eighteen months, Prince had lost interest; now *The Gold Experience* was finally out, it was just another contractual obligation. In outstripping *Come*'s performance to hit No. 6 on the charts, however, he could feel vindicated. Although Warner had refused to allow both albums to compete with each other the previous year, The Artist had proven he could outsell Prince.

* * * * *

'Look at Warner,' Prince reflected in 1997. 'I gave them my music for years and they gave me a ton of gold records. Look what I do with them: I just hang them on a wall. They don't make me happy.' From the moment Prince signed to Warner Bros, he demanded artistic freedom; almost two decades later, his happiness depended on having the freedom to make his own business decisions. As 1995 drew to a close, he officially notified the label of his intention to leave. Although Warner Bros 'never, ever, ever considered dropping him', according to Marylou Badeaux, they eventually consented to let him go of his own accord. 'At some point it was like, "Alright, fine,"' Jeff Gold says. 'We've got his great records in the catalogue. This is becoming too expensive – riderless horse.'

With legal representation from L. Londell McMillan, and help from Russ Thyret, who had advanced to executive-level status since bringing the teenage newcomer to the label back in 1977, an agreement was made that Prince would deliver two albums' worth of unreleased material and accept a reduction on advances from royalties. After signing, on 26 April 1996, Prince declared that he and Warner Bros were 'on the most amicable terms we've been on for a long time'.

That July, Warner Bros released *Chaos and Disorder*. The first album of their agreement included a clear message in the liner notes: having been intended '4 private use only', the collection served as 'the last original material' Prince had recorded for the label. 'It started out with a lot of anger,' Michael Bland says. 'We didn't know at the time that they would concede.'

Described by Prince as an attempt to see 'how fast and hard we could thrash it out', the album was a mix of unused tracks and a few new recordings that leaned towards back-to-basics rock. If the optimistic title track that opened his debut album, *For You*, had presented his music as a gift, *Chaos and Disorder*'s closing song, 'Had U', was his bitter goodbye. While performing the album's only single, 'Dinner with Delores', on *The David Letterman Show* during release week, Prince wore the 'slave' make-up for the last time. 'I was bitter before,' he told the *Los Angeles Times*, 'but now I've washed my face, I can just move on. I'm free.'

9

Emancipation Proclamation

Having severed a business partnership estimated to have generated $300 million between both parties, Prince committed to a more emotionally nourishing relationship. Five years to the day after they met, while Mayte was in Barcelona helping The New Power Generation promote their second album, *Exodus*, he had proposed over the phone. 'We'd never talked about marriage or kids,' Mayte says. 'Something must have happened … He sounded so sure. And for him to speak of that – he's not kidding.' Newly engaged, Prince 'completely changed … He was always very protective and loving, but it was like that final wall was down.'

'I want a big wedding – not a lot of people, but I want it to be memorable,' he told Mayte. Tasking her with hiring a wedding planner, he promised to 'take care of everything else'. 'Normally the bride is like, "OK, this is what we're doing,"' Mayte says. 'No. *He* was the one.'

The following Valentine's Day, 14 February 1996, the couple married at Minneapolis's Park Avenue United Methodist Church – Mayte in a white dress tailor-made by the Paisley Park wardrobe team, Prince in a white suit with a bolero jacket – with Mayte's parents and sister in attendance, along with Prince's mother, stepfather and

Bernadette Anderson, the family friend who had taken the young Prince in during his teenage years. His father, despite living in Prince's old Kiowa Trail house, was not on the guestlist.

Over half a million dollars' worth of flowers adorned the small church – white and gold orchids, gardenias and roses – and a wedding programme was handed out, emblazoned with the question 'Coincidence or fate?' Prince 'wrote that whole programme' while drawing on their meditative discussions, Mayte says. 'It has to be a fate thing. It has to be a past life. Has to be a soul-searching.' Following a private dinner held for family and close friends at Paisley Park, the soundstage was thrown open for a party attended by over a thousand friends, fans and co-workers, with Versace loaning more outfits for the evening.

When, in November 1995, Mayte released her solo album, *Child of the Sun*, a largely dance-pop confection that flirted with her Latin American heritage, it had included a gender-swapping answer to 'The Most Beautiful Girl in the World', 'The Most Beautiful Boy in the World'. Three months later, after years of discussing their metaphysical journeys, it was as if their souls were fusing: the newlyweds' wedding china had an insignia that merged the Love Symbol with the letter 'M'. 'He called that symbol our family crest … He was completely joining me with him,' Mayte says.

Back home, in the Galpin Boulevard house that they now shared as husband and wife – painted white and gold following the nuptials, with a matching BMW Z3 parked outside – the monogram adorned curtains, napkins and towels. 'I feel like she was either my sister or we were the same person or something in another life,' Prince later told Oprah Winfrey. To *Harper's Bazaar* he revealed, 'Mayte grounds me. She doesn't try to change me, but she makes me aware of certain things.'

He needed that kind of influence. 'When we got married, he really did want to have a family and not do anything and just go with whatever came,' Mayte says. She quickly fell pregnant. Nurseries were installed at Galpin Boulevard and Paisley Park – toys, clothes, books and a crib in the former; blue and pink walls, a mini basketball hoop in the latter. In between recording new songs, the couple prepared for a home birth. 'When you have a childhood where you're treated a certain way, you want to treat your child differently,' Mayte says. 'And I know that he wanted that really bad.'

Putting these feelings into song, Prince recorded material for what would become *Emancipation*, his first album release without a major record label's backing – and, largely, without the band that had supported him through the Warner Bros crisis. He'd given The New Power Generation their pink slips – 'Literally, pink slips,' Michael Bland says. After the strain of the previous years, they had become 'a little subordinate', standing up to him over decisions they didn't agree with, 'knowing it would cost us our jobs eventually'.

Relations had been particularly tense since January, following a performance at the start of a seven-date Japanese tour. 'We hadn't been in rehearsal for four weeks,' Michael Bland says. 'We were rusty. Some things happened. I didn't think the show was mincemeat.' A 'hostile' Prince cancelled their pre-gig communal prayers and stopped talking to the band altogether. After turning down an offer to play Australia for a million dollars a show, he suggested the group might want to think about doing something on their own. Then, just days after receiving cheques for the *Exodus* album, they were gone.

'I see in retrospect that it was the kindest way he could do it,' Michael Bland says. 'He made sure we had money in the bank, and that we had prior notice.' But 'the party line coming out of Paisley was that ... he had gone as far as he could go with us musically ... Like we were insufficient ... It had nothing to do with the music. We knew what we were doing.'

Under pressure to prove he could handle all aspects of his business and still turn a profit, Prince had begun taking medication for heart palpitations. After Mayte helped renew communications with his father ('They just were two hard-headed guys ... I saw a big smile on his face when his dad came'), one visit from John L. increased Prince's agitation. Just days before signing his agreement with Warner Bros, security guards rushed him to Minneapolis's Fairview Southside Hospital. Underslept, and after a typically light dinner during which he mixed red wine with his medication, the man who barely touched alcohol had been found passed out on the floor, next to his own vomit; emergency personnel pumped his stomach and gave him charcoal treatment. Prince claimed to have just had a migraine: too many aspirins. 'He was really good at just brushing it off,' Mayte says. 'He didn't make a big deal about it, so I didn't make a big deal about it.'

Soon, Mayte herself was in hospital, suffering complications with her pregnancy. In May, while in New York for the premiere of *Girl 6*, a Spike Lee movie with a soundtrack comprised of old Prince songs, she was taken to hospital with a miscarriage scare; the placenta was beginning to tear away. Appraised of the risks to her pregnancy – the child could be born with dwarfism – the couple were resolute: 'If there's something wrong, we're gonna love it anyway. Let's just have faith.'

In September, two months away from her due date, Mayte began having contractions. Medication kept the birth at bay, but the baby's measurements were so large, doctors informed Mayte that going into labour would kill her. By the time their child, Amiir – Arabic for 'Prince' – entered the world, a month early, on 16 October, Mayte had been in hospital for six weeks, caught in a 'push and pull' between Prince and the medics. 'He wanted me home and I couldn't go home,' Mayte says. 'Every time I tried to get off the medication, I would go into labour.'

The night before the operation, her body 'gave out'. Delivered via an emergency caesarean section, Amiir was born with Pfeiffer syndrome, a genetic disorder that leads to the premature fusion of the skull, as well as abnormalities in the hands and feet. 'It was horrible, yet beautiful,' Mayte says. As her son was rushed to life support, Prince was by Mayte's side: 'He comforted me. We prayed.' Amiir underwent twenty operations before Mayte, bedridden from blood loss, could see him; Prince 'had taken care of all of that'. But with their son suffering, just a week after he had entered the world they were forced to make a decision from 'that ultimate love of: let him go'.

'We never mentioned the word "death",' Mayte says. 'And he said, "We have to bring him back." That was the only thing that kept me going: "Yeah. We have to do that. We have to bring him back."'

* * * * *

Mayte had first heard the song 'Friend, Lover, Sister, Mother/ Wife' at her wedding. By the time it was released, closing the second of the three discs that made up *Emancipation* – where it sat just after a song called 'Let's Have a Baby' – Amiir had been dead for a month. After spending a day grieving with his wife, Prince threw himself into his work. 'He just couldn't handle it,' Mayte says. 'It was the worst thing that ever, ever, ever, ever, ever happened to him … I don't think he dealt with it correctly. I don't think he ever mourned it.'

Determined to make a success out of his first post-Warner Bros album – a triple-disc set, the likes of which his former label had rejected a decade ago – Prince, still identifying as the Love Symbol, set out on an aggressive promotional campaign. 'This is my debut,' he told *USA Today*. 'My name represents this body of work, not what came before.' But *Emancipation* was often given over to celebrations of married life and antic- ipation of fatherhood; one song, 'Sex in the Summer', even featured Amiir's heartbeat, recorded during an ultrasound. After returning from a Japanese promo trip, he filmed a video for 'Betcha by Golly Wow!', a cover of a Philadelphia soul hit made famous by The Stylistics, in which he enacted rushing to Mayte's bedside – at the same hospital in which Amiir was born – to receive the news that she was pregnant.

In reality, his wife was at home, in bed with their child's ashes, cradling an urn decorated with three dolphins

– mother, father, child. Inviting Oprah Winfrey to Paisley Park, where he showed her the newly installed nursery – whose contents Prince would later have burned, along with Amiir's ashes – he deflected the presenter's gentle prodding regarding the health of his child: 'It's all good, never mind what you hear.' Obfuscating further, he added, 'Our family exists. We're just beginning it. And we've got many kids and a long way to go.'

Dazed and grieving, Mayte was roused and brought in front of the cameras. 'The only way he got me in that car was to tell me that we were going to try again,' she says, adding, 'We're finally a married couple and this horrible travesty happens and I've also got to remember that I love this man.' Instructed not to say anything about Amiir, and feeling like a corpse made up for public viewing, she tried not to have 'a complete breakdown' while Prince credited her with helping him 'come closer to who I aspire to be'. 'She makes it easier to talk to God,' he explained.

'He was just letting her know: we're good,' Mayte says. 'We're gonna bring our child back. And he wanted everybody to know that.' Without breaking the news of Amiir's death themselves, however, the tabloids made the couple's loss public: 'Delivery Room Tragedy for Prince: Rock Star's Baby Has Horrible Birth Defect'. Then two former Paisley Park employees, Erlene and Arlene Mojica, twins who had worked for Mayte as nanny and bodyguard, respectively, leaked their own story to the press: the baby hadn't been given enough chance to live; Prince hadn't allowed Mayte to receive the right medical attention; he'd controlled her diet to the detriment of her pregnancy. The Minneapolis homicide department shut it down: the death was due to natural causes. 'There's no case here,' they concluded. The Mojicas were taken to court.

Meanwhile, the verdict for *Emancipation* was largely positive. For every reviewer who felt the album relied on filler to stretch to its three-hour running time, there were others who agreed with *USA Today*'s assessment: 'Artistically, the royal funkster has lost none of his majesty.' Released during a golden age for R&B music, the best of the first disc's slow jams and party tracks showed that, if Prince was no longer setting the pace, he could at least keep up with it. Elsewhere, *Emancipation*'s second disc amounted to a love letter to Mayte, while disc three contained a playful kiss-off to critics ('Face Down') and an impactful R&B-flecked gospel hymn ('The Love We Make') among songs that, at times, tried too hard to prove their relevance, before ending with its jubilant title track.

Calling the album 'probably the most joyous I've made', with songs that were 'by far the most romantic because I've never been this much in love', Prince set off on the twenty-one-date *Love 4 One Another Charities* tour with a new NPG – though, from here on out, each iteration of the group would feel more like hired employees as opposed to the original's ensemble line-up. With Kat Dyson and Mike Scott on guitar, Rhonda Smith on bass and former Game Boy Kirk Johnson on drums, Prince had convinced Morris Hayes to return on keyboards, but Tommy Barbarella turned down a similar invite. 'I jammed for a little bit and it felt so different – not that anyone was bad,' he says. The chemistry had gone. Perhaps to encourage more people to turn out – the shows, running sporadically from January through to June 1997, were not just a promotional tool, but an attempt to raise money for local charities – Prince soon dropped many of the *Emancipation* songs and began relying on his old material.

Despite selling nowhere near two million copies, the RIAA counted each of *Emancipation*'s three sixty-minute discs as a separate unit; by the end of February, EMI, the label Prince had signed a distribution deal with, were celebrating a 'double-platinum' release. When the company went under in the US, the deal came to an end, but Prince 'didn't care', says Hans-Martin Buff, who had become Paisley Park's engineer in the summer of 1996. 'He just got a huge load of cash upon delivery' of *Emancipation*, leading to rumours that the costly deal itself had caused the label to fold.

Prince stayed on the road, launching the *Jam of the Year* tour in July: sixty-five US dates that ran into January 1998 – his longest stretch since *Purple Rain*. With setlists that again relied on his classic hits, the shows pulled in $30 million, rescuing him from the dire financial situation he'd faced just a few years before. Touring for over a year following their son's death, however, he lost the opportunity to grieve together with his wife. On days when he was home, he seemed afraid of communicating.

'I never put any blame on him, but you just start thinking of why this happened and how this happened and stuff that you should talk about as a couple. Things that we didn't do,' Mayte says. She noticed her prescribed Vicodin pills disappearing. At the time, she assumed he was hiding them to keep her from hurting herself; looking back, years later, she couldn't be sure. One night she found spilled wine in the hallway, vomit on the bathroom floor. 'I understood the pills because of our son,' she says. 'I was like, OK, wow. There is a breaking point.' Prince told her, if it ever happened again, she had full responsibility: 'Just take care of everything.' 'For him to do that was a big deal,' Mayte says. It was 'like a promise' that he would never do it again.

'Now I would have taken him and we would have dealt with it,' she adds. But, locked in their private grief, with her husband trying to distance himself from the tragedy, it wasn't a conversation she was able to have. Instead, Mayte bore witness to a series of increasingly intense discussions between Prince and one of his musical idols.

* * * * *

Before Amiir's birth, Prince and Mayte had prayed nightly to God for the safety of their child. 'He was always a religious person, if you listen to his music,' Mayte says. 'He always had a Bible in his bag.' Lost and in search of solid ground, he began to explore other faiths – Buddhism, Hinduism, Judaism, Islam. He and Mayte discussed moving to Egypt; he wanted to know more about how Muslims lived. During an aftershow in the early hours of 23 August 1997, at Nashville's Music City Mix Factory, he met the man who would become the leading spiritual mentor in his life. After inviting Larry Graham, the former bassist for Sly & The Family Stone – inventor of the 'slap bass' technique that came to define funk music – on stage to perform with him, Graham introduced Prince to the Jehovah's Witness faith.

'When Larry started showing up, I noticed a sense of comfort with him,' Mayte says. 'And I remember thinking, This is good. This will cheer him up. It's one of his childhood idols ... But I didn't think we were gonna go out and be Jehovah's Witnesses.'

Soon, Graham and his wife, Tina, were regular guests at Galpin Boulevard. Late-night conversations evolved into intense sermons on the Armageddon and assertions that Christmas and birthdays were pagan ceremonies. Jehovah's Witnesses disavowed medical practices, but Mayte had become pregnant again and wasn't willing to turn her back on medicine. She also refused to raise a child without celebrating its birthday. 'I just couldn't do those conversations,' she says. 'And then I saw the separation ... Women study with women, men study with men.' Telling Mayte to 'talk to Tina about religion', Prince would go to the studio with Larry, 'maybe work on some music and then go *hours* talking'.

Hans-Martin Buff saw another side of their friendship. Larry would be 'so nice to everybody' at Paisley Park 'and give everybody hugs. And that's just nothing that Prince would ever think of,' he says. Prince would ask fanboy questions – 'Did you ever play with Hendrix?' 'Yeah.' 'Did you whup him?' 'Yeeeess' – and would 'roll laughing on the floor' at the answers. During religious discussions, Buff saw Graham 'just alert Prince to the presence of things that he hadn't noticed before', like the nearby Kingdom Hall of Jehovah's Witnesses in Chanhassen. 'I believe that the Jehovah's thing worked pretty well for Prince, because it's clear-cut,' Buff says. 'Prince was a very black-and-white guy, so to have a religion that isn't waffly about stuff ... that made sense to me.'

'I think he thought: if he's in the Witness he was gonna get his baby back,' Mayte says. 'Because he just went full-throttle.' When Mayte began to miscarry their second child, he told her to go to the hospital with Tina; that she 'should naturally let it come out'. Unable to stop bleeding, she went on her own, driven by Prince's chauffeur. 'He just kind of shut down,' Mayte says. 'That's when he got hardcore into his studies.'

10

Over Throne

Unshakeable in his new faith, Prince was also fully committed to running his affairs like a cottage industry. 'There was no large organization in charge of anything,' Hans-Martin Buff says. 'It even went down to that he would sign his own cheques … which made things really hard when he wasn't there and you needed him.' Paisley Park staffers found that if they offered to help with something outside of their remit, it would soon become a full-time responsibility, which is how the engineer came to negotiate the distribution deal for Prince's next album, *Crystal Ball*. 'He put me in a suit and he sent me to Best Buy to sell his record for him,' Buff says. 'With a lawyer, I wrote the paperwork. I did all the back and forth. I organized production of the CD itself.'

Another three-disc set, *Crystal Ball* compiled tracks from the original *Crystal Ball* era of the mid-1980s, plus more recent material. 'He never made a difference between them,' says Buff. 'In his mind, what he did yesterday was just as great as what he did twenty years before … He just wanted to beat the bootleggers.' Prince gave Buff a list of songs to retrieve from The Vault, under the watchful eye of a bodyguard. 'I went through this toyland and loaded up a huge cart … We did a couple of mixes and – bam – it was done.'

If Prince's new music was starting to lag behind the times, his approach to getting *Crystal Ball* to fans was so far ahead of them, it would take the music industry years to catch up. 'I remember sitting in his office in '92, '93, and him saying, "One day, music is going to be sold over the internet,"' drummer Michael Bland says. 'And we hardly knew what the internet was at the time … I left the office thinking he's crazy. Why would anybody want to do that?'

In 1994, on his thirty-sixth birthday, Prince had released the *Interactive* CD-ROM: a computer game that allowed users to explore a virtual world, solving puzzles that unlocked new music. Around the same time, he'd tried to install an internet café, with a touchscreen computer, in his London-based NPG store, but dial-up internet speeds weren't up to the technology. Now *Crystal Ball* was being made available through his website, Love4OneAnother.com, as well as the 1-800-NEW-FUNK number, with Prince telling fans he would manufacture the set as soon as 100,000 pre-orders came in – enough to cover the cost of production, plus some extra for himself. He was just 'testing the water to see if people would buy music over the internet', he told *Guitar World*. Judging the experiment a success, he realized that 'the whole interactive thing offers great possibilities'.

'If you sell it for yourself, nobody can actually check how much you sold,' Buff says, adding, 'The Best Buy thing was by far the biggest part of it all. He got a flat sum from them for *x* amount of CDs that they bought … He made good money.' But if the online venture 'wasn't as big a deal as I think he wanted it to be', it saw Prince become the first artist to sell an entire album through the internet, pioneering a new way of getting his music direct to fans – a no-brainer decades later, when smartphones and high-speed broadband provided online access anywhere, any time, but completely unthinkable in the mid-1990s, when only the most tech-savvy households could access the web. 'He was a total visionary,' says Warner Bros exec Jeff Gold, who had been trying to explore similar avenues at the label.

But it wasn't as easy as it looked. The June 1997 release date came and went, leaving fans waiting until the following January before receiving their copies – if they received one at all. Some had to wait for months; others found duplicate orders arriving in the post. Random customers received additional T-shirts or *Emancipation* lyric books; the promised spherical 'crystal ball' packaging more closely resembled a Petri dish. 'They had to make a mould like you would for an industrial piece,' Buff says. 'It took forever to happen.'

Adding to the confusion, some fans received a promotional cassette featuring a twenty-six-minute song called 'The War' – seemingly unrelated to whether they had ordered *Crystal Ball* or not. Edited down from a forty-minute live performance – and also streamed on Love4OneAnother.com – the song was a stark breakdown of technological, societal and political ills in the run-up to the new millennium.

'It was a failure, but he could see it coming,' Michael Bland says of Prince's ground-breaking trial run. 'He didn't have the manpower or the industry support, and he needed other people in ways that he didn't know yet. But he called that out of nowhere.'

To assuage upset fans who'd ordered *Crystal Ball* directly with him, online orders went out with a bonus disc, *Kamasutra*, an orchestral suite credited to The NPG Orchestra, which had originally been composed for his wedding. All versions of the release included *The Truth*, a largely acoustic album that eschewed the up-to-date production gambits that had defined much of his recent work. 'It became a purpose-laden thing,' Hans-Martin Buff says. 'In the end, I think he thought, this whole concept of acoustic's kind of crappy, and he put all these little keyboard flourishes on there.'

The *NME* called it a 'minor revelation'. Rich in religious imagery, the album offered an insight into Prince's state of mind in the months following Amiir's death, with the song 'Comeback' expressing hopes that he had previously discussed with director Spike Lee: 'If you ever lose someone dear to you, never say the words, "They're gone," and they'll come back.'

If banking on older material was a safe way to test the waters now that he'd added distribution to Paisley Park's business plan, *Newpower Soul*, credited to The New Power Generation, had been a harder sell. 'I think he just saw it as a throwaway,' Buff says. 'And then he popped "The New Power Generation" on it and all of a sudden it was a New Power Generation album.' A diminishing-returns attempt to court a contemporary R&B market, only a hidden track, 'Wasted Kisses', offered much of note: a bitter three minutes featuring ambulance sirens, anguished screams and a flat-lining EKG machine. Meanwhile, Prince asked Mayte to direct the video for 'The One', a song in which he professed his commitment to her.

Whether it was a last attempt to connect through their art, or a parting gift at the end of the road, 'The One' could not save their marriage. The *New Power Soul* and *New Power Soul Festival* tours found Prince playing with more vibrancy than he mustered for their namesake album, but instead of being on the road with him, Mayte was largely annexed in their new home in Marbella, Spain. 'He literally had me empty out the house in Minneapolis and take pretty much everything,' Mayte says; apart from the furniture, which came over from their Paris apartment. 'I didn't realize what was happening until a couple of months after me staying and him not showing up.'

Meanwhile, guests Chaka Khan and Larry Graham travelled everywhere with Prince. He had recorded new albums for both artists – Khan's *Come 2 My House* had followed *Newpower Soul* in September, and *Graham's GCS 2000* was due in February 1999 – but a tone of desperation crept into interviews, as Prince tried to make NPG Records work without the leverage of an established label. He implored radio stations and record stores to 'take care of' Chaka. He boasted of Larry Graham's musical prowess – his mentor was 'Michael Jordan on the bass … how do you not stock that if you love music?' But the music itself didn't often feature in the conversation. When Prince wasn't challenging business moguls, he and Larry were quoting scripture to talk-show hosts who just wanted to keep things light. One of their sticking points was contracts: 'The prefix of "contract" is "con",' Prince would state, explaining the way he was doing business these days – handshake deals, no signed agreements.

Distanced from Mayte, he'd rediscovered another binding document he no longer agreed with: their marriage certificate. Increasingly believing that Amiir's death had been a punishment from God for the life he used to live, Prince felt that their union, too, failed to uphold God's ideals. In the car on their way to a press conference in Madrid, on 11 December, he told Mayte of his plans to announce the annulment of their marriage: they would get baptized together and renew their vows the following Valentine's Day.

'It was a complete disconnect,' Mayte says. 'It was his way of saying, "If you're not going to join me in religion, then I'm not going to continue."' That evening, he tried to convince her to sign a piece of paper which had no legal authority, saying she agreed to the idea. 'Every kind of question was in my mind,' she says. 'What happened? What did I do? I wanted to shake him: "I don't understand what's going on." It was very scary.' Prince threatened to leave if she didn't agree; at four in the morning, exhausted, Mayte gave in and signed. 'And then he left!'

* * * * *

'If anybody ever laid claim to a specific year other than George Orwell and 1984, that's him. It was 1999,' Hans-Martin Buff says. With that year approaching, Prince's old label saw an opportunity to capitalize on one of his biggest songs, sending promotional copies of '1999' out to radio stations to encourage airplay. Prince was incensed – but Warner Bros still owned the master tapes, so he couldn't stop them. 'I was faced with a problem,' he told *USA Today*. 'But "pro" is the prefix of problem, so I decided to do something about it.' Sticking seven newly recorded versions of the song on an EP, he got *1999: The New Master* into stores the following February.

Next, he claimed he would re-record his entire Warner Bros output: 'Two catalogues with pretty much the same music – except mine will be better,' he said. ('The only other thing that happened was a very brief attempt to do a drum'n'bass version of "Let's Pretend We're Married",' Buff recalls.)

Such threats were followed by a slew of lawsuits against fanzines and websites, claiming breach of copyright for publishing the Love Symbol and accusing them of profiting from bootlegged material. Fearing the websites would draw attention from his own activity, Prince also sought to downplay the release of *The Vault... Old Friends 4 Sale*, which Warner Bros issued in August 1999 as their second contractually agreed album. Compiled with little care three years earlier, its mix of jazzy off-cuts and scrapped material from the *I'll Do Anything* film were 'some songs from a long time ago', he told *Rolling Stone*. 'That's not who I am.'

Meanwhile, Clive Davis, the renowned label exec who had signed Janis Joplin, Pink Floyd and Bruce Springsteen to Columbia Records, and launched the careers of many other legendary acts, had recently taken one of Prince's heroes, Carlos Santana, back to the top of the charts. The carefully crafted *Supernatural* album had enough of the Mexican-American guitarist's trademark Latin rock – and a guest spot from Eric Clapton – to appeal to his original fanbase, while also making room for hip-hop producers The Dust Brothers, and rappers Lauryn Hill and CeeLo Green, increasing

Santana's relevance to a new generation of fans. As head of Arista, the label that had issued *Supernatural*, Davis felt he could do the same for Prince's next album.

Prince seemed to agree. 'He wouldn't say it that way,' Buff says. 'But it was pretty clear to all of us – both in the choice of label, Arista, and in some of the things we did when the album came together – namely all the duets – that it was inspired by the Santana album.' Privately, Prince told arranger and NPG trombonist Michael B. Nelson he'd recorded his 'next *Purple Rain*': *Rave Un2 the Joy Fantastic*, for which he had been given an $11 million advance and allowed to keep his master tapes ('It's like going back to school and knowing that you don't have to stay,' he told *USA Today*). Having teased that the album would have a guest producer, in August he finally revealed their identity: Prince. 'He did know how to play the game,' Buff says. 'I liked his humour. He was a funny guy, and I thought that was a really cool thing to do.'

With a new millenium approaching, Prince had wondered what his old self – 'a really good editor, a good decision maker' – would sound like now, he told the *Inquirer*. When the album followed, in November, fans could hear for themselves. The Linn LM-1 drum machine's trademark sound defined some cuts, including the title track, exhumed from the original *Rave Unto the Joy Fantastic* project of 1988; guest artists propped up others – among them Public Enemy MC Chuck D, in an attempt to give 'Undisputed' some hip-hop credibility, and No Doubt frontwoman Gwen Stefani, aiming to bridge the gap between Prince and the younger alt-rock audience.

The album's only commercially released single, 'The Greatest Romance Ever Sold', sat among other lovelorn songs that Mayte felt were aimed at her. He knew she could dance, he taunted, but did she know why Adam *really* never left Eve? The song's video found him cavorting with a performer from Le Crazy Horse, a Parisian cabaret bar Mayte once had to endure a visit to. 'My heart got ripped out of my chest,' she says. 'It was like: is this what you think? … I couldn't believe they had made me out to be the bad person … Just because I wouldn't join your religion, I'm now ousted?'

'Tell me that's not a hit,' Prince had practically ordered *The New York Times*'s Anthony DeCurtis.

It wasn't.

'I always thought if *Rave Un2 the Joy Fantastic* would have been maybe slightly differently assembled – definitely better promoted, with more of a plan – that could have been substantial,' Buff says. But 'he wasn't talking very much in the *Rave* times' and turned down 'huge' offers for projects that could have capitalized on Prince's claim to the year 1999 as the millennium drew to a close. 'Because he was so good, he thought that he deserved to be successful. And I think it irritated him that that just didn't happen.'

'This is a man who is bringing the state of music further along,' Davis had announced before *Rave Un2 the Joy Fantastic*'s release. But the true innovators at the end of the 1990s were Southern hip-hop producers such as Timbaland and the Pharrell Williams-led Neptunes duo, who, between them, had crafted hits for the likes of Jay-Z, Missy Elliott and Kelis, and would soon be all over the charts. Retooling what they had learned from Prince's ground-breaking 1980s work, they pointed to the future of pop music in the twenty-first century. Meanwhile, a song he'd written almost two decades ago held more relevance than anything Prince had released in the 1990s. The *NME* began to wonder if he 'hadn't been killed at the turn of the decade', his record label keeping it a secret while they 'released off-cuts from his previous sessions as new albums'.

'The experiment, in hindsight,' says Hans-Martin Buff, was: 'We'll try the proper classic Prince thing, but just to see: "How can I ride this wave?" Then it's more like: "Fuck it. I'll do my own thing … This is my circus. Follow me if you want to."'

11

Kingdom Come

I t had become increasingly quiet around Paisley Park.
'He wasn't letting people in, even to fix the gear,' Michael
B. Nelson says. What staff remained 'had a tough task
because he kept making them do more … He didn't trust
many people. He just wanted that small little world.'

Launching a new website in February 2000,
NPGOnlineLTD.com, Prince offered his dwindling fanbase
new music and videos for download. He also posted slights
against Arista, along with updates on new projects that
never came to fruition – an upbeat collection called *High*;
a seven-CD *New Funk Sampling Series* containing over seven
hundred snippets of songs for DJs and producers to use.
'I think he realized at some point that he would have had
to give more than he was willing to give, and to relinquish
control that he didn't want to relinquish,' Hans-Martin
Buff says. 'Rightfully so. I don't see the point of doing that
as an established artist.'

The internet was perfect, Alan Leeds, former head of
Paisley Park Records, noted, 'for a somewhat reclusive artist
who enjoys contact with fans under the guise of anonymity'.
But what if he was slipping into obscurity? He'd received
a letter from Mayte in March: they hadn't spoken about the
annulment or the renewal since that night in Madrid ('Like

a lot of things in life I don't like, I pretend it isn't there and it goes away,' he had since reflected).

Now she wanted a divorce. Finalized in May, she got the house in Spain, but little else. That same month, Prince staged a press conference in New York. His publishing deal with Warner Chappell Music had expired at the end of 1999; having reclaimed the rights to his songs, he revealed, 'I will now go back to using my name instead of the symbol I adopted as a means to free myself from all undesirable relationships.'

'I was a bit disappointed when he actually changed back,' Buff recalls. 'I always thought that symbol thing was just a logical conclusion of the conversion of Prince Rogers Nelson, from north Minneapolis, to that thing – fully elaborated.' Calling out 'Prince!' after a conversation, Buff waited to see what would happen. 'There was a brief interval of, "Oh, I guess that's legit now" … and he just went, "Yes?"'

The Artist Formerly Known as Prince was once again officially known as Prince. Now he just needed to create some excitement. Having already shelved a teased Revolution reunion album, *Roadhouse Garden*, the previous year ('What happened was exactly like *Crystal Ball*,' Buff says. 'I went to The Vault and I grabbed the respective songs … As far as a reunion? None of that'), Prince now turned down a lucrative offer to recapture the glory days with a Revolution tour. Instead, he opened Paisley Park's doors for the *Prince: A Celebration* event.

Starting on 7 June, his forty-second birthday, and culminating a week later with a show at Minneapolis's Northrop Auditorium, he staged live performances, let fans take daily tours throughout the complex and asked them to vote for songs to include on a proposed *Crystal Ball II* collection. A twenty-date tour followed, with a new band playing his old hits 'for the last time'.

The shows were a success, inspiring a second run in April 2001, the same month that Prince released a remixed version of *Rave Un2 the Joy Fantastic*. Sent out to members of his latest online fan club, the NPG Music Club, *Rave In2 the Joy Fantastic* replaced 'Strange But True' and his cover of Sheryl Crow's 'Everyday is a Winding Road' with the more downbeat 'Beautiful Strange', and included alternate versions of other album tracks. For a yearly fee of $100, NPGMC subscribers would also receive an array of songs, videos and live performances, along with a series of hour-long Prince- and related-artists-stuffed radio shows, the *NPG Ahdio Show*. He also gave the controversial file-sharing platform Napster a new song, 'The Work Part 1', a month after the service had been ordered to stop users from sharing copyrighted material. Once again, the internet was offering great possibilities.

The kind of work Prince was talking about became clear that June when he staged a second *Celebration* event at Paisley Park. 'I want to put the words "Jesus Christ is the son of God" on the screen and let them deal with it,' he told director Kevin Smith, who had been invited to film the proceedings, which included guest performances and the unveiling of new music. Meanwhile, planned group discussions would allow him to 'talk about religion and lead that into race and lead it into the music biz and radio, and basically at the end of the week I want to change the world'.

His new album, *The Rainbow Children*, was the musical counterpart to this manifesto. Ranging from anywhere between fifty-four seconds to over ten minutes, its warm, organic-sounding songs found Prince at his most engaged in years. Woven from James Brown-indebted funk ('The Work Part 1'), gospel ('Last December'), fusion jazz ('The Sensual Everafter') and even Gilbert & Sullivan-styled opera ('Wedding Feast'), *The Rainbow Children* attacked slavery and systemic racism while also proclaiming Prince's faith louder and more assertively than on any other album. With '1+1+1 is 3' he even rebuilt his old 'Erotic City' motif in pursuit of a different kind of tryst: the only ménage à trois he'd consider these days would involve God.

Reflecting his devotion to the 'New World Translation of the Holy Scriptures' version of the Bible, as favoured by Jehovah's Witnesses, the album told the story of The Rainbow Children, true believers who are penned in by a Digital Garden constructed by The Banished Ones out of 'lies' propagated by the media. In a slowed-down voice, the antithesis of his hypersexed Camille alter ego of the mid-1980s, Prince narrated The Wise One's defeat of The Banished Ones and The Rainbow Children's door-to-door recruitment of like-minded believers willing to help dismantle the garden. He also found space to give The Wise One a love interest, guiding her to revelation while slipping the brazenly sensual 'Mellow' in under the guise of reaching spiritual ecstasy.

Premiered at the June *Celebration*, the album challenged fans' faith – not only in God, but also in their former pop idol. Both musically and thematically, *The Rainbow Children*'s sixty-nine minutes packed in enough ideas for several albums (in 2004, Prince had artwork created for an unreleased sequel), but while many fans were thrilled by a record that found him following his own path rather than chasing trends, others struggled with his unyielding commitment to the Witnesses' doctrine. For most of his career, his relationship between religion and sexuality had been a conundrum; now surrendering himself to the former, he seemed to have given up trying to solve it.

Even more concerning were some of *The Rainbow Children*'s lyrical assertions: obedience to a theocratic order that placed women below men (and all below God); suggestions that Black slaves suffered more than Jewish victims of the Holocaust. This was two decades but entire personalities away from the permissive utopia envisioned on *Dirty Mind*'s 'Uptown'. For Prince, however, the Bible had become 'a history book, a science book' and 'a guidebook to help men and women with their sins'. If he needed relationship advice, he wanted it from Solomon – 'the guy who had a thousand women!'

Critics were as extreme in their responses to *The Rainbow Children* as the album was in its views: for *USA Today* it was 'one of Prince's most challenging and fascinating works to date, whatever your take on the enigmatic valentines to God'; the *Boston Globe* declared it his 'most consistently satisfying' album since *Sign o' the Times*. *Rolling Stone*, however, felt it was 'a long trudge across the desert' with 'Freak-in-the-Pulpit leading the way, waving his synthesizer of holy justice'. Distributed by Red Line Entertainment, *The Rainbow Children* became Prince's first album since his debut not to even enter the Top 100.

* * * * *

Whether or not he could lead his fans to church, Prince was ready to lead his new wife-to-be down the aisle. Eighteen years his junior, Toronto-born charity worker Manuela Testolini had been fundraising for various organizations in the late 1990s, and could occasionally be found posting comments on the fan website alt.music.prince when she first came in contact with him. Representing a Toronto women's shelter in need of financial aid, Testolini was shocked when Prince's Love 4 One Another charity 'saved the day'. Soon hired to work for Love 4 One Another itself, Testolini also became Prince's guest during Bible studies. She received thanks in the liner notes to *Newpower Soul*, while Prince began encouraging Mayte to wear her hair curly – like Manuela's ('The crazy things you tolerate when you're in love,' Mayte, who was 'very aware' of Manuela, says. 'It's a lot of disbelief – this is not happening').

'She was there,' Hans-Martin Buff says of Manuela's ascendance. 'And then she became something that she wasn't before.' Noting that she was 'helpful in getting things done in a good way', Buff adds: 'She was supportive of him, but she wasn't drinking the Kool-Aid. She was a huge fan and she really enjoyed him both as an artist and as a person. But she also saw the bullshit.'

By 1999, Manuela was designing candles and other products for the NPG brand. But where Prince had lived much of his first marriage in public, his second would be a far more private affair. He and Manuela purchased a house in her hometown, on the aptly named Bridle Path.

Relatively remote, midwestern Minneapolis had always offered a privacy he wouldn't have enjoyed in Los Angeles or New York, where the entertainment industry thrives – 'It's so cold, it keeps the bad people out,' Prince said – but Toronto, whose winters were less harsh, was at an even greater remove.

The couple married on New Year's Eve 2001 at the Jehovah's Witnesses' Kingdom Hall in Chanhassen, Minnesota, within easy distance of Prince's mother, who was under observation at Fairview Southdale Hospital in nearby Edina, suffering from long-standing arthritis and kidney problems. The ceremony was 'exceptionally exciting', church elder Ronald Scofield said, because Prince 'was someone who has made a lot of changes to their life'.

Allegedly, one of Mattie's final wishes had been to see her son married and committed to the Jehovah's Witness faith. Just two months after Manuela and Prince said their vows, dressed in robes and immersing themselves in a small pool of water as part of a baptism ceremony held before one hundred and sixty-seven parishioners, Mattie died, on 15 February 2002, at the age of sixty-eight. Her death came just five and a half months after John L.'s, who had died, aged eighty-five, of undisclosed causes, on 25 August 2001.

Relations with his father had always been strained. Sometimes, giving his work the exposure it would never otherwise have received, Prince incorporated John L.'s piano instrumentals into his own songs, as with a passage he transposed to guitar for 'Computer Blue'; other times, as with credits for 'The Ladder' or 'Christopher Tracy's Parade', Prince seemed to be attempting to reach out. He was 'prone to giving people songwriting credit on songs as a way of thanking them', Susan Rogers says. 'It was a way of providing a little bit of money.'

Despite having kicked the young Prince out of his home in the 1970s, John L. had been living in his son's former house and fitted for clothing by Prince's tailors; that Prince felt filial responsibilities towards his father was never in doubt. Their on-off relationship, however, meant that any number of issues may have lain unresolved between them. As with Amiir's nursery, Prince had the house demolished in 2003.

The month after his mother's death, Prince launched the *One Nite Alone...* tour, which lasted until November and took in the US, Canada, the UK, Europe and Japan – his longest trek since rolling the *Love 4 One Another Charities* tour into the *Jam of the Year* shows. 'For those of you expecting to get your "Purple Rain" on, you're in the wrong house,' he warned audiences, but fans were thrilled with his new band, which included a returning Rhonda Smith alongside drummer John Blackwell, trombonist Greg Boyer and keyboardist Renato Neto. A revolving cast of saxophonists made guest appearances, among them long-time collaborators Eric Leeds and Candy Dulfer, and former James Brown sideman Maceo Parker. Wearing tailored suits in sober colours, the group deftly built upon *The Rainbow Children*'s jazz underpinnings, using them as a basis for rearranging select older material.

Capturing some of the intimacy of each night's solo piano slot, a *One Nite Alone...* studio album, subtitled *Solo piano and voice by Prince*, was sent out to NPG Music Club members in May. While some songs seemed like sketches, others were more fully formed; recorded in the spring of 2001, towards the end of the *Rainbow Children* sessions, such ballads as 'Have a Heart' and a cover of Prince's long-standing Joni Mitchell favourite, retitled 'A Case of U', made the album feel like a companion to 1998's *The Truth*. 'Avalanche', meanwhile, took its lead from some of *The Rainbow Children*'s thematic concerns, claiming that Abraham Lincoln never truly wanted to abolish slavery, and using record producer John Hammond – who had helped the careers of such jazz icons as Count Basie and Billie Holiday – as a proxy for the wider music industry's indenture of Black artists.

If the double-disc *One Nite Alone... Live!* (paired with *One Nite Alone... The Aftershow: It Ain't Over!* to create a three-CD box set) gave fans a selection of tour high-lights when it was sent out in November 2002, a brace of studio albums released the following year may have more closely reflected Prince's grieving process. With titles such as 'Xcogitate' (explained in the artwork as 'To consider or think (something) out carefully and thoroughly') and 'Xogenous' ('Derived or developed from outside the body; originating externally'), the all-instrumental *Xpectation* had been recorded in the months following John L.'s death.

Nodding to the 'Directions in music' tagline that began to appear on Miles Davis's albums in the late 1960s, the album offered nine 'New directions in music from Prince': a mix of pensive instrumentals and mid-tempo jazz recorded with his band and featuring some keening overdubs from classical violinist Vanessa-Mae. Released on 1 January 2003, without a physical counterpart, *Xpectation* was one of the first download-only albums ever issued; it was followed by a string of largely instrumental soundcheck recordings named for the cities they were performed in – Copenhagen, Nagoya, Osaka and Tokyo – along with a soundcheck rendition of 'Empty Room', an unreleased song that dated back to 1985.

That summer, the *N·E·W·S* album followed a similar template. 'Directed by Prince', it was recorded with touring bandmates John Blackwell, Rhonda Smith and Renato Neto, plus Eric Leeds, in one single February session, just a month before Prince pulled down the Kiowa Trail house. Each of *N·E·W·S*'s four wide-ranging tracks, 'North', 'East', 'West' and 'South', ran to exactly fourteen minutes, traversing meditative guitar extemporizations, Middle Eastern soundscapes and a fusion sensibility that was even more attuned to jazz and exploratory instrumental music than his *Madhouse* albums of the 1980s.

The record earned a Grammy nomination for Best Pop Instrumental Album – Prince's first Grammys acknowledgement since *The Gold Experience* and 'Eye Hate U' received nods in separate R&B categories almost ten years earlier. But Prince would create a far greater talking point by the time the ceremony itself came around in March. After spending the early 2000s releasing increasingly obscure work with little concern for mainstream appeal, he was ready to make himself heard again.

12

The Comeback Kid

'When you get past the initial shock of actually meeting Prince, he is very persuasive,' church elder Ronald Scofield effused. 'He uses the scriptures very well.' Prince may not have enjoyed the same level of fame as he had in the 1980s – or even the 1990s – but he had been content living a quieter married life with Manuela, shuffling between Galpin Boulevard in Minneapolis and the house in Toronto. He could attend family events, like his new sister-in-law's wedding in the skiing village of Calabogie, Ontario, and be treated like one of the clan.

Back in Minneapolis, he even performed Jehovah's Witness 'field service' duties, rolling up to houses in a black van, knocking on doors with Larry Graham, asking to discuss his faith with residents. 'Cool, cool, cool,' thought one Eden Prairie local, Rochelle, when Prince and Larry approached her front door. 'He wants to use my house for a set.' But then 'they start in on this Jehovah's Witnesses stuff', she recalled. Rochelle and her family were Jewish; it was hours before the start of Yom Kippur, the most important event on the Jewish calendar. 'Can I just finish?' a 'very kind' Prince asked when she protested. After twenty-five minutes and a reading from Larry, they left a pamphlet, returned to the truck and drove off. 'It was so bizarre, you would have just laughed,' she said.

Soon Prince would remember the audience that *was* waiting for him.

* * * * *

On 8 February 2004, in a sign of things to come, he performed at the Grammys, opening the event with Beyoncé. Trading vocals with the future Queen Bey shaking it like Tina Turner by his side, Prince made peace with his hits in public, playing 'Purple Rain' with an orchestra before blasting through 'Baby I'm a Star', a snatch of Beyoncé's 'Crazy in Love' and his own 'Let's Go Crazy'. In a fitted purple suit with a gold shirt and matching pocket hankie, he switched from his purple Love Symbol-shaped guitar to his decades-old Hohner, throwing the latter to the floor as he teased the audience: 'Don't hate us 'cause we fabulous.'

On 15 March, he was inducted into the Rock and Roll Hall of Fame, confirming his legacy in the eyes of the industry he had spent a decade trying to dismantle. His induction was 'automatic', says former Warner Bros Senior Vice President Bob Merlis, then on the voting committee. 'You wouldn't have to think twice about that.' The ceremony was another tear-up: 'Let's Go Crazy', 'Sign o' the Times', 'Kiss', with a second appearance later that evening.

As part of an all-star tribute to the late George Harrison, Prince stood alongside Tom Petty, Jeff Lynne, Steve Winwood and Harrison's son, Dhani, who all watched on as he made Eric Clapton's iconic 'While My Guitar Gently Weeps' guitar solo his own. Standing at the side of the stage, set designer Roy Bennett, who, ten years after leaving the fold, had enjoyed 'a really heart-to-heart, beautiful' hour or so with Prince earlier in the day, recalled, 'You could see 'em: they're so in awe that they're laughing, because it was just like, "Oh my fucking word." They were blown away.'

'After a decade spent tending only to his faithful,' *Time* magazine noted, 'Prince has had a revelation: he's supposed to be a rock'n'roll star.'

'I get asked every year to play at the Grammys,' Prince shrugged. This time he agreed as a way of promoting his new album and tour. *Musicology Live2004ever* once again promised all the hits for the last time (though it was 'called the *2004ever* tour', Prince deflected, adding, 'And time is forever'), and also gave fans the *Musicology* album.

Launching a download store of the same name on 24 March, Prince made the album available for purchase along with two volumes of NPGMC tracks, *The Chocolate Invasion* and *The Slaughterhouse*, plus *C-Note*, which collected 2003's stand-alone soundchecks. He wasn't trying '2 make other labels nervous', Prince said of allowing fans to download his new album for $9.99 before it was even released in the shops (where it would be sold for up to twice as much). He just needed 'a worldwide distribution service that works as fast as we do'.

Fans who bought tickets for the tour – arena shows performed on an X-shaped stage in the round, which delivered all the promised hits along with intimate solo acoustic performances and even some support slots from The Time – also received the album as part of their ticket purchase.

But Columbia Records, who were releasing *Musicology* the traditional way in April, as a joint NPG Records release, weren't fazed. Despite competition from Prince's methods of getting the ablum into fans' hands – or on their computers – Don Ienner, the president of Sony, Columbia's parent company, claimed the label made money 'with the first copy shipped'.

Effectively pre-echoing reviews of every Prince album to follow, *Musicology* was either his most 'appealing, focused and straight-up satisfying' album in years (*Rolling Stone*), or a record that offered 'a handful of old tricks, but no new ones' (*The New York Times*). But to Prince, its twelve songs were 'more or less a companion to the concert'. Exploiting a loophole in the way Nielsen SoundScan registered sales in the US, every ticket purchased for shows after *Musicology*'s 20 April street date would count as an album sale. Eight years earlier, Prince had suggested to *Forbes* that he could give fans 'the whole thing and build it into the ticket price'. Now, he noted, 'If I sell 400,000 tickets to my shows, that would make me No. 1 on the charts before I even release a CD into record stores.'

It didn't go that far. *Musicology* peaked at No. 3 in the US (and matched that performance in the UK, where there was no accompanying tour), but the promotional gimmick once again challenged industry norms. One unnamed label executive bemoaned a future where 'a dinosaur act that no longer sells records but does great live business can do a stadium tour over the summer and dominate the *Billboard* 200', maintaining, 'The charts are supposed to represent what consumers are spending money on. With the Prince album, there is no choice.'

By the end of 2004, *Pollstar* had named Prince the highest-grossing musician of the year, earning over $87 million from the tour alone. *GQ* magazine crowned him Funkmaster of the Year. *Billboard* honoured him for Best Use of Technology. Nielsen SoundScan, however, amended the way they counted sales. From now on, customers had to be allowed to opt out of any album-ticket bundles.

Journalists called it a comeback; Prince balked at the word: 'I never went anywhere!' But this besuited – and contented – Prince felt new to reporters who had become accustomed to his antagonism. While he continued to urge fans to let God guide them through the purple rain, he'd eased up on the hardcore proselytizing. His concerts and new music could still be sensual, but they were never lewd: swearing was off the cards; songs like 'Darling Nikki' had been retired. Prince was trying to 'put the family first', he told reporters. He'd come to an age where he had 'certain responsibilities to deal with'. Besides, he asserted to *Newsweek*, 'When I was making sexy tunes, that wasn't all I was doing. Back then, the sexiest thing on TV was *Dynasty*, and if you watch it now it's like *The Brady Bunch* ... There's no more envelope to push. I pushed it off the table.'

* * * * *

If Prince felt there were no more boundaries to break in his music, *Musicology* marked the first in a run of albums with which he would explore new marketing techniques. After a quiet 2005, on 13 December he announced *3121*, to be released in partnership with Universal. When asked by veteran reporter Barney Hoskyns why he now seemed to be joining 'the biggest slavery ship of them all', Prince demurred: 'I don't consider Universal a slave ship.' He'd gotten 'exactly what he wanted' out of the deal, structuring it 'the way I saw fit instead of the other way around'.

Prince also brought a new protégé to the label, Támar Davis. But after happily playing a sideman role on guitar throughout her showcase tour, he decided to take centre-stage again. Davis's planned album, *Milk & Honey*, slipped from the schedule as *3121* hit the shelves, on 21 March 2006, and ran through the usual touch points – playful electro-funk seductions, quiet storm ballads and pop-rock throwbacks, along with a judicious use of family-friendly innuendos.

Although failing to 'create something fresh and contemporary' from 'his 80s bag of tricks', as *Entertainment Weekly* observed, a 'Purple Ticket' campaign helped the album go straight to No. 1 in the US – his first No. 1 album since *Batman*, and his first ever to debut at the top of the charts at home – as fans sought a handful of Willy Wonka-style invitations to a private show at Prince's rented LA mansion at Sierra Alta Way on 6 May.

Eighteen days later, Manuela filed for divorce. After finalizing an agreement in October 2007, the courts sealed the documents; ten years later, the Minneapolis *Star Tribune* had them unsealed in a freedom-of-information request. Among details of a lavish lifestyle that included accounts at Gucci, Versace, Valentino and Saks ('There was never any restriction' on their spending), $5,000-a-day stylists, $15,000-a-night hotel suites and

$50,000 parties, it was also revealed that the couple sought relationship counselling from Jehovah's Witness elders based in New York.

The exact reasons behind their divorce were not recorded in the documents, but, during a year in which Prince spent most of his time in Los Angeles, a May 2005 incident shed light on the state of their relationship: Prince had locked Testolini out of the Galpin Boulevard house, cut off her credit cards (seeking a $42,574-a-month allowance in the settlement, she initially came away with a $10,000 monthly support, a Lexus, a $3 million transfer to her company, Gamillah Holdings Inc., and the house in Toronto), boxed up her belongings and stowed them in Paisley Park for 'safe keeping'. The property then became the second former home that Prince demolished.

In public, he was served awards, not divorce papers. 'Song of the Heart', written for the animated children's movie *Happy Feet*, received a Golden Globe. On 12 June 2006, he was given a Lifetime Achievement Award at the tenth annual Webby Awards, with Webby founder Tiffany Shlain praising 'a visionary who recognized early on that the web would completely change how we experience music'. Three weeks later, after receiving a trademark infringement suit from the Nature Publishing Group, Prince pulled the plug on his NPG Music Club. It had 'gone as far as it can go', he wrote in a statement.

The 'online magazine' 3121.com briefly took its place: new tracks and photos followed, along with reports on what was happening during the *Per4ming Live 3121* residency that Prince staged at Las Vegas's Rio All-Suite Hotel and Casino.

Settling into the hotel's top suite that November, he kicked off a run of Friday- and Saturday-night shows that extended through to April 2007. 'It's pretty much the Prince world brought to Vegas!' stage dancer Maya McClean said: fans could 'really experience what it's like to be in Prince's home'.

Rebranding the Rio's nine-hundred-seat venue Club 3121 and selling tickets for upwards of $125, Prince performed intimate early-hours sets that had more in common with his aftershows than the recent hits-filled *Musicology* tour. After finishing in the main venue at close to two in the morning, he'd often appear an hour or so later at the smaller 3121 Jazz Cuisine restaurant. For $312 a ticket, fans would receive a bottle of champagne, dinner cooked by Prince's personal chef, Lena Morgan, and be within touching distance of the star as he ran his band through unpredictable setlists, lost in music until gone 5am.

* * * * *

It didn't rain much in the desert, but it was lashing down in Miami on 4 February 2007, when Prince, a marching band and his current NPG line-up performed at the Super Bowl XLI halftime show. Miami was so weather-beaten that day 'it was like a scene from *Moby-Dick*', production designer Bruce Rodgers recalled. Knowing he would deliver the performance of a lifetime before one hundred and forty million viewers, Prince had one request: 'Can you make it rain *harder*?'

On a Love Symbol-shaped stage, set up in seconds in the middle of the field, he ran through 'Let's Go Crazy', 'Baby I'm a Star' and 'Purple Rain', plus a snatch of

'1999', while also claiming Queen's 'We Will Rock You', Creedence Clearwater Revival's 'Proud Mary', Bob Dylan's 'All Along the Watchtower' and Foo Fighters' 'Best of You' as his own. Clad in purple, the Florida A&M University Marching Band came out on cue. The rain continued to pour.

A truly independent artist calling everything on his own terms, Prince still carried all the clout of a major-label headline act. The most-televised event of 2007 seemed to have been the only way to top the Grammys and Rock and Roll Hall of Fame ceremonies. But when Prince arrived in London that May, to announce his *Earth* tour, he had a record-breaking residency in his sights: twenty-one nights at the city's 24,000-capacity O2 Arena, to run throughout August and September.

Concert promoter Rob Hallett recalled telling Prince they could do twenty-one nights in the city, 'just as long as you're prepared for the last ten days to be in Ronnie Scott's', a small jazz club in London's Soho district. Prince, however, 'wouldn't even consider the possibility of anything else'. Pricing general-admission tickets at £31.21, Prince ensured that each night was a sell-out. Performing nightly aftershows at the complex's smaller IndigO2 venue encouraged UK and European fans to keep returning.

As with *Musicology*, his new album, *Planet Earth*, was given away with each ticket, but when Prince also sold it to the *Mail on Sunday* newspaper, which bundled the CD with their 15 July edition – marking the first time a brand new album had been released as a free covermount – a day before his new label partners, SonyBMG, were due to release it in stores, SonyBMG reportedly tore up their contract. It was 'ridiculous' to have a UK deal, an employee said, when millions of copies were being given away for free.

Prince turned this back on them: 'Were you planning to sell three million copies in London?' he asked. 'I sold three million copies overnight.' He also pocketed anywhere between £200,000 to £500,000 from the *Mail on Sunday*, while giving the paper its best-selling issue since Princess Diana's death. Some estimates had Prince making over eight times the amount that he had from *3121*'s UK sales, even though the cost of promoting the partnership allegedly left the *Mail on Sunday* losing money.

If *Planet Earth* was the sound of Prince 'trying a little harder than usual', according to *Rolling Stone*, the *Earth* tour – rebranded *21 Nights in London* – gave a total of 504,000 casual fans the hits they wanted to hear. His most devoted supporters, however, came under fire as Prince enlisted Web Sheriff, an online-policing firm, to issue take-down notices to fan-run websites that posted photos from the shows. The Warner Bros battle of the 1990s had 'left its scars, but it also made him a lot more savvy in terms of protecting his rights', the company's founder, John Giacobbi, told TheRegister.com. That was about physical releases, he continued, 'and now that we're into the digital age, he's fighting for his online rights'.

Forming the PFU coalition (for PrinceFansUnited.com – or: P: F-U!) in November 2007, the fan websites hoped to negotiate terms that would allow them to continue operating. A draft agreement was never signed, but Prince sent the collective a song to stream online: 'PFUnk'. An update of a track recorded during the *Musicology* sessions, it warned of digital music's impermanence and cautioned fans to stop antagonizing him. Received as his most inventive seven minutes since *The Rainbow Children*, the song was renamed 'F.U.N.K.' and soon appeared on iTunes, for official download.

Prince's own photos of the London residency, collected in the *21 Nights* coffee-table book, along with the *Indigo Nights* CD – a document of his O2 aftershow performances – served as an official souvenir for London-based gig-goers. In the US, the three-disc set he had prepared as part of an exclusive deal with Target stores, whose headquarters was based in Minneapolis, should have brought him into millions of homes across the country. But a damaging interview distracted from all that.

In November 2008, just weeks after California had passed its Marriage Protection Act – known as Proposition 8 – which formally declared, 'Only marriage between a man and a woman is valid or recognized in California,' *The New Yorker*'s Claire Hoffman asked Prince about his views on same-sex marriage and abortion. Tapping his Bible, he told her: 'God came to the earth and saw people sticking it wherever and doing whatever, and he just cleared it all out. He was, like, "Enough."'

Despite having built his career on demands for freedom – creative, intellectual, sexual – and presenting an androgyny that had helped countless members of an oppressed LGBTQ+ community find their own voices, Prince had failed to rally for the cause when many public figures were declaring their allegiance. Faced with a backlash, he claimed he was misquoted. Hoffman herself noted that he was 'a true believer', and that readers should keep that in mind: 'the way he said it wasn't hateful so much as sad and resigned', she observed.

Prince sought to divert attention to his forthcoming release, inviting journalists to his newly rented property on 77 Beverly Park Lane for private playbacks. Blasting from his car as he drove each guest around Hollywood, *Lotusflow3r* was exploratory rock in the *Rainbow Children* mode. Back at the mansion, and previewed in a black sports car christened 'Miles Davis', *MPLSound*'s electro-funk revisited the 'Minneapolis sound'.

Premiered in a bedroom setting, *Elixer*, the debut album by his latest protégé, Bria Valente, was, in Prince's words, 'nasty, but not dirty music' (when the collection was released in March 2009, her effort was received as 'a throwaway, done as a favor for a friend'). He appeared on *The Tonight Show with Jay Leno* for three consecutive nights, and also stopped by *The Ellen DeGeneres Show*, giving copies of the three-disc package to everyone in the audience and – on air, at least – gifting his guitar to the host, arguably the most prominent lesbian in the US and a vocal critic of Proposition 8.

Target's footfall of thirty million customers a week helped take the collection to No. 2 on the *Billboard* 200 and No. 1 on the Top R&B/Hip-Hop Albums charts, but the distribution deals were losing their spark. The *20Ten* album, released in the summer of its namesake year, felt dated the moment it slipped out from select newspaper supplements in the UK and Europe. A lyric that referenced threats from Saddam Hussein, the Iraqi leader hanged in 2006, suggested a disconnection from reality – even while Prince had very real-world considerations on his mind. 'Self-interest is on the back burner for now,' he told *Ebony* magazine. 'There is too much at stake.'

13

Compassion Projects

'Prince was never there when you did not need him,' says Van Jones, a former Barack Obama advisor turned CNN commentator, and the co-founder of non-profit organizations such as Dream Corps. 'He was always there when you did.' He also felt 'it was literally against his religious teachings to take any credit at all for his public good works. He spoke often about how disgusted he was by people who were giving away money and naming buildings after themselves.'

But as Prince set out on a string of tours under the *Welcome 2* banner, taking in the US, Europe, Canada and Australia, from December 2010 through to May 2012, Jones began to see that 'he wanted to do more and say more'. Feeling 'handcuffed' by the Jehovah's Witnesses' 'anti-politics', Prince used the shows as an opportunity to be more public about his philanthropy. 'It wasn't the first time that he was using his presence in cities to help people, or giving proceeds from concerts to local charities,' Jones says. 'That was the first time he started doing it a little bit more visibly.'

Even while Minnesota's *Chaska Herald* reported, in March 2011, that Prince seemed in danger of defaulting on a mortgage loan, he had donated $1.5 million to the New York groups Harlem Children's Zone, American Ballet Theatre and Uptown Dance Academy. In an email interview with *Time Out Chicago*, on the eve of a three-night run in the city, designed to raise money for Van Jones's Rebuild the Dream project, Prince noted that church congregations were asked to clean up after meetings, leaving buildings in a usable state for their next occupants. 'We feel the same way about this country,' he wrote. 'Shouldn't we try 2 leave it in a better shape than when we found it?'

On a global scale, annual donations were being made to Physiotherapy and Rehabilitative Support for Afghanistan, among other charities the scope of which may never be known – many recipients of his philanthropical gestures were placed under strict non-disclosure agreements. 'He was always prowling the internet,' Jones says. 'He would look for emergency situations – medically or even legally … Like if you knew somebody who it seemed was being treated unjustly and they needed a lawyer or may have had some kind of costs.'

After the fatal shooting of a seventeen-year-old Black teenager, Trayvon Martin, in 2012, Prince contacted civil-rights activist Al Sharpton in order to get financial aid to Martin's family – unbeknownst to the recipients. When Black Lives Matter launched in 2013, in response to the acquittal of Martin's killer, George Zimmerman, an anonymous Prince was one of the organization's first donors.

'Publicly, he's always been more mixed-genre, mixed-constituency,' Jones says. 'Privately, he was very concerned about what was happening to the Black community.' Feeling that he had benefited from local music-based initiatives launched by community centres such as The Way, Prince asked Jones,

'Where's the musical programme for the creativity of today – computers and coding?' Noting that, 'When a Black kid is seen wearing a hoodie, people assume, Oh, there goes a thug; but when a white kid is seen wearing a hoodie, people assume, Oh, there goes Mark Zuckerberg,' Prince challenged Jones: 'Maybe we haven't created enough Mark Zuckerbergs. Maybe we need to be focused on that.' Giving Jones funds for a new venture, #YesWeCode, he sought to help provide disadvantaged communities with education in digital technology.

'He always felt himself being allied with the youth,' Jones says. 'Probably the biggest insult from Prince you could possibly get was, "That sounds old."'

Youthful new talents also fell under his purview, as Prince scoured YouTube in search of promising young artists whose careers he could elevate. 'If he found some four-year-old who was playing the violin, he would reach out to the parents,' Jones says. 'He really wanted to make sure that musical prodigies got good parenting. That the parents got good advice ... "This kid is going to need this kind of parenting, this kind of mentorship."' He also sought to expand his own roster of protégé acts, overseeing *Superconductor*, the second album by Andy Allo. Ranging from assured, playful numbers of her own ('People Pleaser') to intimate acoustic ballads co-written with Prince ('Long Gone', 'The Calm'), the album was largely recorded during downtime in Zürich's Powerplay Studios in August 2011 and finished back at Paisley Park early the following year.

According to his sometime internet mouthpiece Dr Funkenberry, Prince had taken 'a musical liking ...

and perhaps other likings' to the vivacious, talented multi-instrumentalist after she joined his band as a guitarist in 2011. But by the time *Superconductor* was made available for download, on 20 November 2012, Allo had left The NPG. Still constantly recording – one engineer told arranger Michael B. Nelson that he had completed six albums in seven months: 'They're all done and put away. And they're all different' – Prince hadn't released a new album in two years. And then, suddenly, it seemed as though someone else was threatening to do it for him.

* * * * *

On 31 December, a figure calling themselves 3rdEyeGirl drew attention to their YouTube account by posting a 'leaked' new song, 'Same Page Different Book'. Posing as an 'international art thief', 3rdEyeGirl soon began sharing remixes and rehearsal footage of Prince with his new band – an all-female trio featuring Texan newcomer Hannah Ford-Welton on drums, Ida Nielsen on bass and flourishing Canadian bandleader Donna Grantis on guitar – across Facebook, Twitter and SoundCloud. Following a cease-and-desist letter from Prince's lawyers – also gleefully posted across social media – the songs were removed.

'We were just goofing around,' Ford-Welton later said. During breaks from twelve-hour rehearsal sessions, six days a week at Paisley Park, the group would play ping-pong, eat pancakes – Prince's latest favoured food – and 'make these mysterious videos'. They 'didn't know it was actually maybe part of a plan'.

During a 1 March performance on *Late Night with Jimmy Fallon*, Prince officially revealed 3rdEyeGirl's identity: the three musicians he was now playing with as part of a stripped-down funk-rock quartet that were rearranging – and revitalizing – his back catalogue. He then took the group on a string of club appearances: eighteen dates, two shows a night, largely along the US West Coast on what was dubbed the *Live Out Loud* tour. Early Prince biographer and *Star Tribune* music critic Jon Bream felt he'd seen 'the most exciting Prince show' since the *Sign o' the Times* era of the late 1980s. Without even releasing an album, Prince and 3rdEyeGirl commanded headline slots at summer festivals; *Rolling Stone* hailed them as the second-greatest live act in the world. 'It seemed like almost a family thing,' says Michael B. Nelson. 'He took those girls under his wing.'

Saying goodbye to the US with a surprise appearance on TV sitcom *New Girl*, Prince popped up in the home of London-based soul singer Lianne La Havas, for what he playfully called *The Living Room Experience*. Sipping tea and dismissing the thirtieth anniversary of *Purple Rain* ('I hadn't even realized') before a handful of journalists, he announced an open-ended *Hit and Run* tour: small venues, with a view to working 'our way up, if people like us'. Announced at the last minute, with tickets initially starting at just £10, the shows had fans queuing for hours in the hopes of getting into intimate clubs such as Camden's Electric Ballroom and the 2,000-capacity O2 Shepherd's Bush Empire.

After a year on the road, 3rdEyeGirl were a tighter unit – 'an all-girl blitzkrieg', in *Clash* magazine's view, with, in *The Guardian*'s estimation, 'a galaxy-class showman playing like a band with a residency in a local bar'. *Hit and Run Part II* tour – larger venues, more notice; a handful of shows in Europe – followed during the summer, but a bigger surprise was in store: Prince was about to make peace with his most bitter adversaries.

Having come into effect in 1978, the year that Prince released his debut album, the Copyright Revision Act of 1976 allowed for the termination of copyright grants after a thirty-five-year period. Authors of a work could now demand the return of their rights after this time frame. It had yet to be tested in court – according to *Billboard*, many labels were 'unsure how copyright terminations and ownership revisions would play out' – but, eighteen years after his split from Warner Bros, Prince seemingly, finally, owned his master tapes. He then re-signed with the label in a deal that gave them distribution rights to his music, while he retained full ownership of his work.

An announced *Purple Rain* reissue missed the album's anniversary but, two decades after struggling to control Prince's work rate, Warner agreed to release two of his albums on the same day: *Plectrumelectrum*, recorded with 3rdEyeGirl, and *Art Official Age*, a solo album with, for the first time ever in Prince's career, a co-producer, Hannah Ford-Welton's husband, Joshua Welton.

Pieced together throughout much of the previous year, *Plectrumelectrum* – named after an instrumental written by Donna Grantis – failed to capture the energy of the group's live shows. *Art Official Age* felt more considered. Joshua Welton's EDM production style may not have made for a natural fit on some tracks, but the album's stand-out moments encouraged *The New Yorker* to greet it as 'easily' Prince's 'most coherent and satisfying album in more than a decade'.

Framed by a loose concept in which its creator is placed in suspended animation for forty-five years while undergoing affirmation therapy, songs like 'Breakdown' and 'Way Back Home' reckoned with the passing of time, standing as mature works from an elder statesman in a reflective state of mind. Thirty-seven albums into his career, and after years of seemingly defying the ageing process, Prince was facing up to his mortality and exploring new ways of navigating the world.

* * * * *

Having worked with Prince throughout the 1990s, during his most fraught professional dealings and darkest personal tragedies, Michael B. Nelson, now back and arranging material for an array of projects, among them new 3rdEyeGirl songs and Prince's latest protégé release, Judith Hill's *Back in Time* – a versatile debut that touched upon vintage jazz, classic R&B and early 1970s Sly Stone – often found him 'in a state of joy', no longer so 'isolated'. Less hands-on than he had been before, Prince would 'just kind of pop in and out, check in on things – and he'd throw some curveballs that would really trip you up … It was really fun to have those moments with him in those last years and really feel more of a connection and warmth, because when he was happy and having fun, it was really nice to see.'

In January 2015, Prince presented a Golden Globe to rapper Common and R&B singer-songwriter John Legend; their song 'Glory', penned for the Martin Luther King, Jr., civil-rights movie *Selma*, had won Best Original Song. The following month, he handed Beck the Album of the Year Grammy for *Morning Phase*. Sporting the afro he'd grown out in recent years – challenging his childhood hairstyle for size – Prince told the assembled artists and label executives at LA's Staples Center: 'Like books and Black lives, albums still matter.'

'He was moving more in a direction of feeling like he needed to be more outspoken about the causes of injustice – especially racial justice,' Van Jones says. Although 'not somebody that was going to be able to hold forth on the details of 1960s politics or Thurgood Marshall's arguments before the Supreme Court', or looking to 'spend a whole bunch of time trying to dig through all the details', Prince 'cared about politics in the more modern sense' and 'could see through the bullshit'. 'Where he planted his flag was Africa,' Jones says. 'He was fascinated by the glory days of ancient Africa: the big library at Timbuktu; he was fascinated by Amarna.'

Having once treated the Bible as his only guidebook, now he was studying Afro-centric interpretations of history, the physics of sound, Egyptology and Eastern philosophies. 'It's just all expanded,' he told *Rolling Stone* of his self-education, before bringing up a series of grievances: when President Kennedy was assassinated – before he could pass the Civil Rights Act – his car slowed down ('Why doesn't it speed up?'); AIDS was on the rise in some communities, not others

('Any primate could figure out why'); chemtrails – something that had been on Prince's mind since 2008 – continued to trouble him ('Think about *where* they appear, *why* they appear, how often and what particular times of the year').

And then Freddie Gray died in Baltimore, on 19 April. Many music fans had been busy celebrating that year's Record Store Day; Prince had staged a Record Store Weekend Jam at Paisley Park that same night, in support of local Minneapolis outlets like Electric Fetus. The twenty-five-year-old Gray, meanwhile, had been in a coma, having suffered spinal-cord injuries during his arrest. The medical examiner ruled another young Black male's death a homicide.

A week later, when Fox 9 journalist Iris Perez arrived at Paisley Park, Prince was on the soundstage, recording with 3rdEyeGirl. During conversation, he was visibly emotional – one of his biggest inspirations, Joni Mitchell, had recently been hospitalized with a brain aneurysm. But that wasn't the real reason for the session. 'With everything going on this week, I had a lot I needed to get out,' he said. His new song, 'Baltimore', namechecked both Michael Brown and Freddie Gray, and ended with a chant that referenced the slogan 'No justice, no peace'. In the early hours of the following morning, Prince re-recorded the song on his own. Three days later, he opened the doors to Paisley Park, staging a Dance Rally 4 Peace in order to raise funds for Baltimore, which had been beset by riots. Attendees were asked to pay $30 a head and to wear something grey.

After streaming the new song for free on 3rdEyeGirl's SoundCloud account, in advance of another fundraiser, the Rally 4 Peace, held at Baltimore's Royal Farms Arena, Prince gave it to hip-hop mogul Jay-Z's streaming service, TIDAL. The company also streamed an hour of the Baltimore show, matching fans' $17,323 donation to raise $34,646 for the Open Society Institute of Baltimore. Prince himself gave money to several other programmes: NAACP's Afro-Academic, Cultural, Technological and Scientific Olympics, Baltimore's YouthWorks and OneBaltimore.

Refusing to deal with the prominent Apple Music and Spotify platforms ('Why should Steve Jobs get my money when he can't even play guitar?'), Prince also gave TIDAL his first new album of 2015, *HITnRUN Phase One*. 'He loved TIDAL. He loved Jay-Z because Jay-Z did what Prince wanted to do,' Jones says. 'Prince put his music on the internet first ... but he never could figure out the business side.' Still 'most passionate' about artists 'owning their own everything', Prince saw Jay-Z as a 'great hero' for controlling the technology behind the service.

'Privately, he was very explicit on the racial analogies, in terms of: We're on the plantation,' Jones says. 'They – the white executives, the white music industry, the white media companies – still see us as slaves on the plantation. We do all the work, and they get all the money. He saw Jay-Z and TIDAL as being a huge exception to that rule, and that's why he was so excited about it.'

Released just months apart, in September and December, respectively, *HITnRUN Phase One* and *HITnRUN Phase Two* again presented opposing sides of Prince's music. With more EDM experiments from Joshua Welton, some recent singles gathered in one place and interpolations of *Art Official Cage* material, *HITnRUN Phase One* succeeded more as an addendum than a stand-alone record. Noting its title, Pitchfork.com felt the album didn't fulfil 'the possibility of a concept worth serializing', though *The Guardian* called it 'the enduring classic we've been waiting for'.

HITnRUN Phase Two – the final album credited to Prince & The New Power Generation – was a more organic-sounding band work. Cherry-picking from one-off tracks that didn't fit *HITnRUN Phase One*, it was, in *Vanity Fair*'s estimation, 'a grab bag tribute to Black music of the 1970s'.

* * * * *

'He was just in a flow,' Michael B. Nelson says of Prince's work rate during the decade. 'The floodgates seemed to open up – maybe it went back to normal at that point.' Rehearsals with a new band were defined by the sound of bassist MonoNeon as Prince tapped into early jazz fusion, working his way towards a planned new project, *Black is the New Black*. More 3rdEyeGirl material was also being recorded. Nelson had been asked to orchestrate Prince's guitar solos for strings, woodwind and brass instruments – as he had with 'Baltimore' – for a project that Prince hoped would help 'reinvent the Minneapolis sound' with cinematic songs recorded with an orchestra. 'What he was digging about that stuff,' Nelson says, was 'the way vibrations work with a real string section or real orchestra'.

In one unreleased song, 'Grace', Prince sang of being on a mountaintop with the wind around him; looking back on his life, he is astonished at what he sees. 'I tear up listening to that,' says Nelson. But Prince 'just kind of dismissed it …

I expected him, for some reason, to open up a little because that tune was so reflective.'

And yet Prince had been in a reflective mood. In March 2016, he announced that he was writing a memoir, *The Beautiful Ones*, for Random House. The publishers had made 'an offer I can't refuse' for a book that Prince envisioned as 'starting right at the beginning with my first memory' and going through to the Super Bowl. In conversations with his editor, Dan Piepenbring, the book could have juxtaposed moments from his past against experiences in the present day. Or it could have been about how the music industry worked. Or about his mother's role in his life. In one discussion, he aspired to 'write a book that solves racism'.

Most nights, Prince could be found filling Paisley Park's soundstage with the sound of his piano, playing alone until the early hours of the morning; sometimes he would repeat three seconds of a song, over and over, until he felt he'd perfected them. Focusing so intently on the instrument was an attempt 'to challenge myself, like tying one hand behind my back, not relying on the craft that I've known for thirty years'.

In January, he'd previewed the *Piano & A Microphone* tour with a 'gala event' at Paisley Park, setting the tone for the shows that followed: ruminations on growing up and learning to play; snatches of TV themes he'd taught himself as a child; praise for those who had helped him, including Wendy and Lisa; setlists that gave rare outings to risqué songs like 'Dirty Mind' and deep catalogue tracks like 'Joy in Repetition', and which, as the tour wound through

Australia and on to California, Canada and Georgia, found him leading crowds through a chant that gave a new song its title: 'Free Urself'. That first night, in Paisley Park, Prince concluded: 'Throughout it all, remaining free, I found out that God was love.'

The *Piano & A Microphone* shows were dedicated to his father, '4 all he taught his musical son'. Mortality was on Prince's mind. One of his first girlfriends from Minneapolis Central High School, Kim Upsher, had died of a brain aneurysm in November 2015. Just before opening the *Piano & A Microphone* tour in Australia, on 16 February, he received news that Denise Matthews – who, as former protégé Vanity, had spent years struggling with drug addiction before finding religion – had died of kidney failure. 'Her and I used to love each other deeply,' he told the audience during an emotional set, dedicating 'Little Red Corvette' to her and changing lyrics to 'The Ladder' to include her name.

Other lost loved ones had been visiting him while he slept: 'Some of my friends have passed away, and I see them in my dreams,' he had revealed to the gala audience in January. 'It's like they are here, and the dreams are just like waking sometimes.'

'I just feel for him,' Lisa Coleman says. 'I think he was really feeling haunted and sort of grieving – I don't know if he knew how to grieve.' Thirty years after The Revolution disbanded, she remained in touch with Prince, but now 'he wasn't communicating'. 'I thought that he was in trouble,' she says. 'I don't think he was communicating to anybody the way he should have … I think that he was just trying to live up to who he was instead of accepting who he needed to be for that time.'

Prince's onstage digressions occasionally took on a confessional tone, as if he were unburdening himself. But he had a secret that only his closest confidants knew. Performing energetic shows, wielding a guitar in his trademark six-inch high heels – steel-reinforced to prevent against their breaking – had become agony. 'Wearing those shoes – he did everything, as everybody knows,' Roy Bennett says. 'Those splits that he did, he would just drop and pull himself back up on his heels … What he put his hips through was unbelievable.' Increasingly reliant on opioids to keep the pain at bay, sitting at the piano night after night offered a way of playing his music in comfort.

But not even girlfriend Judith Hill knew the extent to which he was in pain. 'He was quick on his feet,' she later recalled. 'Never said anything, that this is hurting, never a sign of struggle.'

* * * * *

'We have a major problem. Prince is really sick.' *Piano & A Microphone* tour co-ordinator Kim Worsøe was on the phone to Lucy Lawler-Freas, who had been promoting two shows booked for that night, 7 April, in Atlanta. Prince had 'the flu' and could barely speak after returning from the doctor. 'He's not going to get on the plane and he needs to postpone the show,' Worsøe said.

Throughout the early part of 2016, Prince had 'the flu or a cold, always', his personal chef, Ray Roberts, later told *City*

Pages. Recently, however, Prince had been 'off his game and needed to rest. I had to be careful about what I was serving him.' Some nights, he would only eat desserts – sour cream apple coffee cake, chocolate mousse, caramel sea salt cake – others, he'd just take one bite of his meal and leave the rest. Prince still 'wasn't feeling well', Lawler-Freas noted, when, a week later, he arrived at Atlanta's Fox Theatre, but he 'gave it his all' throughout both sets. Over dinner, while flying back to Minneapolis in the early hours of the following morning, he passed out.

'His eyes fixed,' Judith Hill later told *The New York Times*. 'We knew it was only a matter of time; we had to get him down.' At one moment, she 'thought he was gone'; they managed to rouse him and get him talking. After an emergency landing at Quad City International Airport in Moline, Illinois, Prince was given an emergency shot of Narcan – used to counteract opiate overdoses – and rushed to Trinity hospital.

'All is good,' long-term aide and sometime New Power Generation member Kirk Johnson told Minneapolis's *Star Tribune* from Paisley Park the following morning. Prince was just suffering from 'bad dehydration'. He'd stayed in hospital overnight but allegedly left in the morning because he couldn't get a private room. Hours later, Prince was on stage at Paisley Park, telling fans, 'Wait a few days before you waste any prayers.' During the short appearance, he unveiled a new guitar (but decided to 'leave it in the case or I'll be tempted to play it') and offered a few instrumental runs on the piano, before leaving the crowd to an excerpt from the second Atlanta show, revealing that he planned to use the recording for a live album.

More public appearances followed: 16 April was Record Store Day, and Prince travelled to Electric Fetus, buying six albums, including Joni Mitchell's *Hejira*, Stevie Wonder's *Talking Book* and Santana's *Santana IV*. Two days later, he was photographed cycling along a Chanhassen bike path. The following evening, he caught a show at the Dakota Jazz Club.

Meanwhile, his aides initiated 'a life-saving mission'. Prince downplayed his hospital visit, but Judith Hill informed Paisley Park insiders of its severity; privately, Prince had become 'serious about getting help' for his addiction. Five days after the Atlanta incident, on 19 April, his team contacted Dr. Howard Kornfeld, a specialist in treatments for chronic pain and substance dependency, who founded the California-based outpatient clinic Recovery Without Walls. Prince was in the middle of a 'grave medical emergency', they told him. Unable to travel to Minneapolis immediately, Kornfeld sent his son Andrew, along with a 'small amount' of Suboxone, a prescription drug used to treat opioid abuse. Prince himself had visited a local doctor, Michael Schulenberg, to undergo some tests. 'He did it because he was concerned, and he wanted to do the right thing for his own body,' Hill recalled. 'And that's the part that breaks my heart, because he was trying. He was trying.'

On 20 April, Prince stopped in at a Walgreens pharmacy near his home. An hour later, he returned to Paisley Park. Ray Roberts had prepared a roasted red pepper bisque with kale salad; he was told to leave it and go. 'He didn't seem like his normal self that night,' Roberts recalled. 'He'd been like that for months.'

The following morning, 21 April, Prince missed his appointment with Andrew Kornfeld, who'd flown in overnight. When Kirk Johnson, Prince's assistant Meron Bekure and Kornfeld arrived at Paisley Park, they found Prince – his clothes on backwards, his socks inside-out – lying unresponsive in the elevator that led to his private living quarters.

With Johnson and Bekure in 'too much shock' to do anything, Kornfeld made the 911 call: 'The people are just distraught,' he told emergency services at 9.43am. 'We're in Minneapolis, Minnesota, and we are at the home of Prince.' Five minutes later, an ambulance arrived, but with rigor mortis having set in – Prince's body had lain undiscovered for anywhere up to six hours – the medical personnel attempted CPR in vain. At 10.07am, Prince Rogers Nelson was officially pronounced dead.

Epilogue: Transcendence

'**You** ain't supposed to die,' Prince told *Ebony* magazine just months before his death. Faith was 'supposed to be like wings. Take you up higher. Now do your work from a higher place, get more done, cover more ground and whoop your competitors.'

Although Prince had once feared dying at the age of twenty-seven, as so many other musicians have, 'He didn't fear death,' Mayte Garcia says. 'His goal was to become spiritually elevated to the point where you've cleaned every corner of your soul, to where you don't have to come back.'

'He really was not completely planted on earth,' Michael B. Nelson says. 'I think he was straddling two realities. He had his anchor into this world, but he wasn't totally there. It was like he was phasing in and out of wherever else he was drawing from.' In the days that followed the news of Prince's death, many fans recalled lyrics in 'Let's Go Crazy', suggesting that he didn't die in that Paisley Park elevator – he just punched a higher floor.

* * * * *

In what his publicist Yvette Noel-Schure described as a 'private, beautiful ceremony' attended by a small group of family, friends and bandmates, Prince was cremated at First Memorial Western Chapel on Sunday, 23 April, and his ashes taken to Paisley Park. At the perimeter of the complex, fans left notes, mementoes, flowers and purple balloons; inside, his two pet doves, Majesty and Divinity, were said to have fallen silent.

A shrine was built beneath Prince's star on the First Avenue wall; on the day he died, 15,000 people had filled a four-block radius around the club for an impromptu tribute party. 'Every institution, every building, every landmark in the city was purple ... It was like the city was glowing, and you could hear Prince music just walking down the street,' says Andrea Swensson, who had spent the day 'standing in the eye of a hurricane', reporting from Paisley Park for Minneapolis public-radio station The Current, and doing live cut-ins as international broadcasters picked up on the news. 'It was so celebratory and so special; it was like a send-off party of: we love you *so* much. And thank you.'

Around the world, major landmarks were lit purple, the Eiffel Tower, Melbourne Arts Center and Empire State Building among them. Prince was added to the Walk of Fame at New York's Apollo Theater, a legendary venue in the history of Black music; NASA honoured his stratospheric achievements by tweeting a photo of a purple nebula in the sky.

Pulling himself out of poverty, pushing his music into new territory, fighting for artists' rights, leading revolutionary changes in the music industry and driving his bands to deliver the best live performances in the world, Prince was always looking to re-evaluate where he was and to take himself in a new direction. But, having spent decades defying limitations, at the age of fifty-seven he eventually came up against them. Known for sustaining days-long recording sessions in his twenties, he had allegedly been awake, working on new projects, for six days straight before he died. The physical demands of his live shows – performing choreographed dance routines, leaping off pianos and drum risers, and dropping into the splits, all in his high heels – had taken their toll.

'He really did push himself to extremes,' Lisa Coleman says. If he ever fell, 'It was concerning,' but 'he'd be OK, dust himself off.' B12 shots would give his body a vitamin boost before hitting the stage for the next demanding performance, but, 'Sometimes, after gigs, he'd be on the floor and they'd be giving him oxygen. It was like being an athlete.'

Although he eventually had a hip operation, his Jehovah's Witness faith had precluded him from seeking proper medical treatment until it was arguably too late. In the final years of his life, Prince relied on opioids to alleviate chronic pain. Counterfeit pills found at Paisley Park had been made to look like Vicodin; they were laced with fentanyl, a synthetic opioid up to a hundred times more potent than morphine. 'In all likelihood, Prince had no idea he was taking a counterfeit pill that could kill him,' Minnesota authorities said. An official investigation concluded, 'Others around Prince also likely did not know that the pills were counterfeit containing fentanyl.' There was 'no reliable evidence' to show how Prince obtained them; no criminal charges were filed.

'He punished his body for decades,' drummer Michael Bland says. 'I saw him do incredible things that humans shouldn't do … Sonny and I would watch him jump off the second tier of the stage, into the splits and come up, and we would just look at each other like, "That dude is out of his mind!"'

'That's what the rehearsals, the practicing, the playing is for,' Prince told *Essence* magazine. 'You work to a place where you're all out of body. And that's when something happens. You reach a plane of creativity and inspiration. A plane where every song that has ever existed and every song that will exist in the future is right in front of you.'

He was, he explained elsewhere, seeking transcendence through his music.

'When that happens – oh, boy.'

A Note on the Text

Chart placements

The US *Billboard* albums and singles charts changed their names with some regularity throughout the years covered in this book. Every effort has been made to reference them correctly, according to their contemporaneous use.

Sources

This book would not have been possible without the input of the people who worked with Prince during his lifetime and who agreed to speak on the record for the project, giving freely and generously of their time, sometimes over the course of more than one conversation and further emails. All quotes in the book from the following sources come direct from conversations with the author throughout 2020, with the exception of Hannah Ford-Welton, who spoke with the author in 2014, for a feature that appeared in *Record Collector* magazine.

Marylou Badeaux
Tommy Barbarella
Brenda Bennett
Roy Bennett
Michael Bland
Hans-Martin Buff
Lisa Coleman
Mayte Garcia

Jeff Gold

Van Jones

Peggy McCreary

Bob Merlis

Michael B. Nelson

Chris Poole

Susan Rogers

Andrea Swensson

Hannah Ford-Welton

The following publications and websites were also invaluable for further research and quotes.

Billboard

Business 2 Magazine

Chaska Herald

City Pages

Clash

TheCurrent.org

Daily Mirror

Details

Detroit Free Press

Ebony

El País

Enquirer

Entertainment Weekly

Essence

Housequake.com

The Guardian

Guitar World

Los Angeles Times
Mail on Sunday
Melody Maker
Minneapolis *Star Tribune*
Minnesota Monthly
Musician
The New York Times
Newsweek
NME
People Weekly
Pitchfork.com
Pollstar
Prince.org
PrinceVault.com
Q
Record Collector
TheRegister.com
Rolling Stone
Salon.com
San Jose Mercury News
Shift
Spin
St. Paul Pioneer Press
Sweet Potato
Time Out Chicago
The Times
USA Today
Vibe
The Village Voice
Wired

There is a growing body of Prince scholarship, to which this book is my third contribution. The following titles are recommended for anyone interested in Prince's life and art. Some laid the foundation stones for the rest of us to build upon; others have furthered our understanding of his continued impact on pop culture.

Mike Alleyne and Kirsty Fairclough (eds), *Prince and Popular Music: Critical Perspectives on an Interdisciplinary Life* (Bloomsbury Academic, 2020)

Marylou Badeaux, *Moments... Remembering Prince* (Memories4You, 2017)

Allen Beaulieu, *Prince: Before the Rain* (Minnesota Historical Society Press, 2018)

Jon Bream, *Prince: Inside the Purple Reign* (Collier Books, 1984)

BrownMark (with Cynthia M. Uhrich), *My Life in the Purple Kingdom* (University of Minnesota Press, 2020)

Morris Day (with David Ritz), *On Time: A Princely Life in Funk* (Da Capo, 2019)

Dez Dickerson, *My Time with Prince: Confessions of a Former Revolutionary* (Pavilion Press, 2003)

Jason Draper, *Prince: Chaos, Disorder, and Revolution* (Backbeat Books, 2011)

Jason Draper, *Prince: Life & Times: Revised & Updated Edition* (Chartwell Books, 2016)

John W. Duffy, *Prince: The First Illustrated Biography* (Omnibus Press, 1992)

Mayte Garcia, *The Most Beautiful: My Life with Prince* (Trapeze, 2017)

Ben Greenman, *Dig if You Will the Picture: Funk, Sex, God and Genius in the Music of Prince* (Faber & Faber, 2017)

Alex Hahn, *Possessed: The Rise and Fall of Prince* (Billboard Books, 2003)

Dave Hill, *Prince: A Pop Life* (Faber & Faber, 1989)

Barney Hoskyns, *Prince: Imp of the Perverse* (Virgin, 1988)

Owen Husney, *Famous People Who've Met Me: A Memoir by the Man Who Discovered Prince* (Rothco Press, 2018)

Liz Jones, *Slave to the Rhythm* (Little, Brown, 1997)

Alan Light, *Let's Go Crazy: Prince and the Making of Purple Rain* (Atria Books, 2014)

Per Nilsen, *Prince: A Documentary* (Omnibus Press, 1990)

Per Nilsen, *Dancemusicsexromance: Prince: The First Decade* (Firefly, 1999)

Per Nilsen and jooZt Mattheij with the *Uptown* staff, *The Vault: The Definitive Guide to the Musical World of Prince* (Uptown, 2004)

Steve Parke, *Picturing Prince: An Intimate Portrait* (Cassell, 2017)

Prince, *The Beautiful Ones* (Century, 2019)

Prince and Terry Gydesen, *Prince Presents: The Sacrifice of Victor* (Paisley Park Enterprises, 1994)

Prince and Randee St. Nicholas, *21 Nights* (Simon & Schuster, 2008)

Ronin Ro, *Prince: Inside the Music and the Masks* (Aurum, 2011)

Afshin Shahidi, *Prince in Hawaii: An Intimate Portrait of an Artist* (NPG Music Club, 2004)

Afshin Shahidi, *Prince: A Private View* (St. Martin's Press, 2017)

Randee St. Nicholas, *My Name Is Prince* (Amistad, 2019)

Andrea Swensson, *Got to Be Something Here: The Rise of the Minneapolis Sound* (University of Minnesota Press, 2017)

Matt Thorne, *Prince* (Faber & Faber, 2012)

Touré, *I Would Die 4 U: Why Prince Became an Icon* (Atria Books, 2013)

Duane Tudahl, *Prince and the Purple Rain Era Studio Sessions: 1983 and 1984: Expanded Edition* (Rowman & Littlefield, 2018)

Duane Tudahl, *Prince and the Parade and Sign "O" the Times Era Studio Sessions: 1985 and 1986* (Rowman & Littlefield, 2021)

Joseph Vogel, *This Thing Called Life: Prince, Race, Sex, Religion, and Music* (Bloomsbury Academic, 2018)

Jim Walsh, *Gold Experience: Following Prince in the '90s* (University of Minnesota Press, 2017)

Robert Whitman, *Prince: Pre Fame* (NJG, 2017)

Stuart Willoughby, *Minneapolis Reign: A Guide to Prince's Hometown* (Sixth Element Publishing, 2017)

Acknowledgements

My first thanks must go to Joe Minihane for suggesting me to Laurence King Publishing, which gave me the opportunity to write this book. I now owe him a barbecued sea bass (if he even remembers what that is a reference to).

Extra special thanks go to my editor, Donald Dinwiddie, whose guidance and patience were invaluable throughout the whole project. Even as the book soared past its planned word count, he encouraged me to keep telling the story in the best way possible – and then helped shape it, making it even better. Thanks also to Marie Doherty, Nicola Hodgson, Felicity Maunder, Florian Michelet, John Parton, Andrew Roff, Charlotte Selby, Gaynor Sermon and Marc Valli for getting it over the line in the final stages. And a special shout-out to Uli Knörzer, whose royally stylish cover illustrations have truly taken the crown.

Lifelong thanks for more than just this book go to my mum, Carol, and my dad, Colin. It was a joy taking dad to see Prince live, but it was even more special to have finally gotten him to a Guns N' Roses concert before he died.

I couldn't have written this without the unending love and support of my wife, Nicola, and our Jack Russell, Chota, who have now had to endure twelve years' worth of the minutiae of Prince folklore (and poor Nic only likes him 'a normal amount').

And, of course, the biggest thanks go to Prince, who really is the person who made this book possible. His artistry truly knew no bounds, and continues to shape our world.

Index

Index

Picture Credits

1. Richard E. Aaron/Redferns/Getty Images
2. Gary Gershoff/Getty Images
3. Paul Natkin/Getty Images
4. Lynn Goldsmith/Corbis/VCG via Getty Images
5. Richard E. Aaron/Redferns/Getty Images
6. Patrick Aventurier/Gamma Rapho via Getty Images
7. Michael Putland/Getty Images
8. Rob Verhorst/Redferns/Getty Images
9. Jim Steinfeldt/Getty Images
10. Entertainment Pictures/Alamy
11. Crollalanza/Shutterstock
12. Gie Knaeps/Getty Images
13. Brian Rasic/Getty Images
14. Frank Micelotta/Getty Images
15. Frank Micelotta/Getty Images
16. Jonathan Daniel/Getty Images
17. Kevin Mazur/Wireimage/Getty Images
18. Cindy Ord/Getty Images